THE VEGETARIAN
IN THE FAMILY

THE VEGETARIAN
IN THE FAMILY

JANET HUNT

Thorsons
An Imprint of HarperCollins*Publishers*

Thorsons
An Imprint of HarperCollins*Publishers*
77–85 Fulham Palace Road,
Hammersmith, London W6 8JB
1160 Battery Street,
San Francisco, California 94111–1213

First published as *A Vegetarian in the Family* 1984
This edition, completely revised and updated, 1994
1 3 5 7 9 10 8 6 4 2

© Janet Hunt 1994

A catalogue record for this book
is available from the British Library

ISBN 0 7225 2859 0

Phototypeset by Harper Phototypesetters Limited,
Northampton, England
Printed in Great Britain by
HarperCollinsManufacturing Glasgow

CONTENTS

INTRODUCTION

Who is this book for?

There are plenty of books about vegetarian food. This is a book with a difference. It shows how vegetarians (or vegans) and non-vegetarians (people who eat meat and fish) can live together in harmony, or something approaching it anyway. This book is for you if you do most of the cooking and someone in your family – a teenage son or daughter, husband or wife, the au pair – has recently become vegetarian, or if a disconcertingly growing number of the guests you invite round to dinner turn out to be vegetarian. It's for you if you're concerned about healthy eating for yourself and your family, and want to – if not change your diet completely – at least slot some vegetarian meals in amongst the others; or if you simply enjoy cooking and tasting different foods and want to experiment with this fashionable and fascinating cuisine for the sheer fun of it. And it's for you, most certainly, if you yourself are the new vegetarian in the family, trying to work out the logistics of sharing a kitchen, Sunday lunch and family life without causing too much disruption to anyone.

In other words, it's for everyone who is in any way touched by a trend that is sweeping the country, affecting restaurants, supermarkets, magazines, airline caterers, schools, just about everyone – the trend towards a vegetarian lifestyle.

Why eat vegetarian?

You may not wish to reduce your own consumption of flesh foods at all, even though you may have to prepare vegetarian dishes for someone in the family. Just the same, it may help you understand his or her feelings if you know what prompted the decision.

The reasons for becoming vegetarian are so varied that people of all ages, backgrounds and lifestyles are being drawn towards this way of eating. Undoubtedly it's healthier. Giving up meat means giving up the saturated fats in meat, not to mention the growth hormones, antibiotics and other additives that are part of today's meat-production industry. Fish are taken from seas into which pesticides, oil, heavy metal, radioactive waste and sewage are dumped. As sea fish supplies dwindle, fish farms are becoming more common, and these frequently rely on the use of hormones and pesticides.

However, it isn't just what's banned from the table that makes a vegetarian diet healthier – it's what fills the gap. Nutritionists around the world are encouraging us to consume more vegetables, fruit, whole grains and pulses, the very ingredients on which the vegetarian diet is based.

Ecologically, too, it makes sense to eat less meat. As the population continues to increase at a staggering rate of nearly 200 people per minute, demand for food becomes ever more desperate. Fattening animals on plant food in order to eat their flesh is one of the most wasteful ways of producing food – it takes ten pounds of grain to produce one pound of beef. Yet a vegetarian world could easily support the current population. It would also reduce the need to chop down rain forests, would mean no more slurry lagoons contaminating the underground water levels from which our tap water is taken, no worries about the spread of diseases such as foot-and-mouth and BSE (mad cow disease). And our housekeeping money would go much, much further!

Concern about animal suffering is another common reason for avoiding meat. Modern farming methods mean that animals such as cows, pigs and sheep lead miserable and entirely unnatural lives, ending in a terrifying journey to the slaughterhouse, and violent death. As more people become aware of the horrors involved, consumption of meat drops. Unfortunately, instead of switching to a more humane system of rearing animals, the farming industry simply spends more money on advertising in an effort to convince an increasingly doubtful public that meat is necessary for life and health.

Whatever reason the vegetarian in your family has for making the decision, be assured that he or she is in no danger of wasting away, losing energy or becoming ill. Quite the opposite, in fact. And having one vegetarian in the house gives everyone else the chance to experiment with this different way of eating.

Is a vegan diet healthy?

The vegan diet, which eliminates all foods of animal origin, may seem inadequate, but far from it. In fact vegans, with their low consumption of saturated fats and high consumption of natural fibre, are following all the advice being given by a growing number of nutritionists without even trying.

When switching to a vegan diet it is important to study the basic principles of nutrition, making sure you are eating enough protein. And although vitamins and minerals are usually abundant in the vegan diet, vitamin B12 (found mainly in foods of animal origin) may need to be supplemented. It is, in fact, often added to commercially prepared vegan foods.

When shopping for vegans, do check the ingredients lists on all commercially produced foods carefully. Polyunsaturated margarines, for example, may sound innocent, yet they often contain whey, a by-product of the cheese industry. Arm yourself with one of the many excellent reference books giving details about additives in foods. Also, check with The Vegan Society for lists of acceptable products.

Though a diet based on plant foods may sound dull, it can be delicious, and much more varied than you'd imagine. There are a number of recipes in this book to get you started (look for those marked V+), and many more can easily be adapted – check the tips given with each recipe for suggestions.

How should you use this book?

Living in a family – or sharing your home with other people, whoever they may be – means first having to accept that everyone is different and then making all sorts of compromises so that there is the minimum of friction. Eating, especially if meals are to be taken together, can be one of the most hazardous areas of family life. This book aims to help vegetarians and carnivores live (and eat) together harmoniously.

The first chapter explains how to set up your kitchen and offers advice on equipment and basic ingredients. Next comes a chapter of answers to the most common queries about vegetarianism, some of them important, many of them seemingly trivial – until they crop up at the most inconvenient moment.

The main section of the book is devoted to recipes that will take the vegetarian through from breakfast to late-night snacks. Some are simple and can be put together in minutes; others are sumptuous dinner-party fare, requiring a little more time and effort. Many of the recipes will probably be enjoyed by everyone in the family, vegetarian or not, and for this reason quantities are enough for four average servings. If you are cooking them for one, either reduce the quantities accordingly or freeze the extra portions for use another time. Many of the recipes also include suggestions on adapting them to suit the non-vegetarians in the family. And that – the mixing and matching of dishes – is what the final section is all about. Here you'll find lists of dishes or types of dishes you might serve to meat or fish eaters, and alongside each one is a complementary vegetarian alternative, which perhaps uses similar cooking techniques or can be served with the same accompaniments. By matching meals in this way you'll keep your kitchen work to the minimum. You'll also enable everyone to share a meal in the true fashion, rather than just sitting down together. And that, surely, is what living together is all about.

BEFORE YOU START

Though there are numerous practical things that can be done to make life easier when vegetarians and non-vegetarians live together, the single most important thing to work on is attitude.

The decision to become vegetarian is rarely taken lightly. It may be made after months or even years of collecting and considering facts. Or it may come as a blinding flash – the result of seeing a film, reading an article, talking to someone. Whatever the reason, and however strong his or her conviction, the new vegetarian will be vulnerable, and if other members of the family tease, or even attack, the sparks may well fly.

Another problem can arise if non-vegetarians in the family feel they are being criticized – either verbally or simply by implication – for not choosing to join in and give up meat. A family at loggerheads is bad enough, but as the one time everyone is likely to meet up is over meals, indigestion may be one thing you all have in common!

It is important, therefore, that everyone is allowed to voice their feelings, their doubts, to ask questions. A younger member of the family might dread missing out on his favourite fish and chips. Someone else might be keen to join in but fear being teased by friends at school. Wage earners might anticipate the housekeeping rocketing. Discuss these things. At least you'll all know where you stand. As any change is best made gradually, you may also find it useful to have another chat later, when the new routine is under way and there may be other problems to be talked over.

A new cuisine

But isn't it all very complicated, all those beans and Japanese foods? It's a familiar question, and one to which the answer is both yes and no. Yes, in that every unfamiliar cuisine needs to be studied before you start. If you planned to cook an Indian meal for the first time, you'd probably read up about it first, then go along to a specialist store and stock up on at least some of the basic ingredients. Take the same approach when you start vegetarian cookery and you'll find it well worth while.

You probably already eat at least a few meatless meals a week without even thinking of them as such. Omelettes, macaroni cheese, vegetable soup, bubble and squeak, baked beans on toast . . . these old favourites can probably be served to everyone in the family. But what about those occasions when you want to serve meat or fish to some members and a vegetarian dish to others? Since the last thing most cooks want to do is prepare two completely different meals, it's a good idea to get into the habit of matching the dishes as closely as possible. For example, if you are serving chops, fry some cheese or tofu for the vegetarian and serve the same vegetables or salad to everyone. Or if you're making a stew, make up the same basic mixture, use two casseroles, and add meat to one and beans to the other. Preparing fish paella? Put a portion of the rice aside before adding the fish, and sprinkle it with nuts.

Look through this book for plenty more ideas on how to cut your cookery to the minimum without anyone in the family having to lose out, then try some experiments of your own.

Setting up your kitchen

You probably already have most of the equipment you'll need: heavy-based saucepans, a set of good-quality knives, a chopping board, a grater, a measuring jug, scales, a steamer so that your vegetables don't lose all their goodness. But there are a few other items that will be especially useful in a house where both vegetarians and non-vegetarians share the kitchen.

SMALL ELECTRIC GRINDER

The kind usually used for coffee beans. It will make light work of chopping up nuts, and is also useful for making breadcrumbs.

WOK

These originated in China where cooking fuels were in short supply, and are designed to use minimum heat while preserving all the nutrients in the food. If you are likely to cook meat or fish in your wok, it is a good idea to get two, either with different handles or in different sizes, or mark one with tape so they don't get mixed up.

SPROUTER

There are various types, but one of the most popular (and inexpensive) comes in the form of three round plastic tiers that slot together. Use it to grow your own sprouts in days – the easiest are mung bean, lentil and alfalfa, though there are plenty of other beans, grains and seeds to try.

PRESSURE COOKER

This will cook beans, grains and vegetables in next to no time. Look out for one made of stainless steel or enamelled steel – they're more expensive but worth it.

SMALL DISHES

Assuming that there is just one vegetarian in the family, do stock up with lots of small dishes in which you can cook individual portions. These can include ramekins, flan dishes, Yorkshire pudding tins and muffin tins. It's also well worth buying some individual silver foil cases which can go from oven to freezer and back again, and, if you're careful, can be re-used time and again.

FREEZER

Though not essential, a reasonably large freezer really will help. You'll be able to prepare extra quantities of slow-cooking beans and grains and freeze them until needed. Try to get into the habit of cooking extra portions when following the recipes in this book (and others). Most prepared dishes can be frozen, and are so useful when time or kitchen space is limited. Careful packing is important. Strong packaging such as thick aluminium foil (or foil cases – see above) is ideal as it helps retain moisture as well as keeping out air. Chill food in the fridge before transferring it to the freezer. If the dish contains pastry it should be frozen uncooked. Sauces, purées and homemade vegetable stock can be stored in ice-cube trays to provide small portions. Don't forget to label everything, noting not just what it is but when it was stored.

MICROWAVE

When microwaves first came on to the market many doubts about this way of cooking were expressed, and with reason. Since then, safety regulations have been tightened, and microwaves are now standard in new kitchens. Though they can be used to cook dishes, they are especially popular as a way of heating up frozen meals, and are invaluable when kitchen facilities are at a premium.

SMALL GRILL

It's possible to buy small, free-standing grills that cook portions for one or two – again, an excellent way to free the main grill for meat dishes. If the small grill is reserved just for vegetarian food, there is no risk of it being tainted with animal fat.

YOGURT MAKER

A yogurt maker is especially useful for vegans, as dairy-free yogurt is often hard to find in the shops yet can be made easily using soya milk.

Ingredients

You'll also probably be familiar with many of the basic ingredients you'll need, though not necessarily in their healthiest form. Why not replace them with healthy or vegetarian ingredients that can be eaten by everyone? Items to look out for include vegetable stock cubes, vegetarian suet, soy sauce, good-quality vegetable oil such as sunflower, olive oil for salads, vegetable polyunsaturated margarine, agar-agar (use instead of gelatine), vegetable yeast extract, wholemeal flour, natural food colouring (instead of cochineal, for example, which comes from insects). Make a point of using these ingredients all the time, whether you're cooking vegetarian food or meat or fish. It'll make your task considerably less complicated, and you'll improve the health of the whole family by using nutritious versions of foods that are all too often refined and/or adulterated with chemicals.

Other basic foods are suggested below. It isn't necessary to buy them all, of course. Just add to them as you go along. As most of them are now available from good supermarkets you should be able to find them easily.

PULSES

These are dried beans and lentils. Use as wide a variety as possible, preferably buying them in small amounts and from shops that have a fast turnover – even though they keep well, the fresher they are the more nutritious they'll be and the quicker they'll cook. Store pulses in an airtight container in a cool place. As they take some time to cook, you might like to keep some cans of ready-cooked beans in stock for emergencies.

GRAINS

Brown rice is the most popular, but do also try bulgur, wheat berries, kasha (buckwheat), rye and oats. These can be whole or flaked, and should be unrefined. Many are available ground into flours, which makes them easy to use but also means they stay fresh for a far shorter time. Corn or maize meal, also sold under its Italian name, polenta, is especially versatile. All grains should be bought in small amounts and stored in airtight containers in a cool place.

PASTA

Pasta is made from durum wheat and comes in more shapes and sizes than you'd imagine possible. Tasty and low in calories, it's also quick to cook and very versatile. Wholemeal pasta contains more fibre, but there's no reason why you shouldn't use refined pasta too every now and then. The coloured varieties are especially attractive – green is coloured with spinach, red with tomato purée. Buy dried pasta or fresh (which can be frozen until needed). Some pastas contain egg – vegans, take care.

NUTS AND SEEDS

Almonds, hazelnuts, cashews, Brazils, pistachios, tiger nuts, pumpkin seeds, sunflower, sesame, alfalfa – all are highly concentrated sources of protein and other nutrients and play an important role in the vegetarian and vegan diet. Though fairly expensive, they only need to be used in small amounts. Peanuts (which aren't true nuts but the pod of a leguminous plant), are the best known and the cheapest. Buy nuts and seeds from busy shops with a quick turnover, and store them in airtight containers. Nuts and seeds keep best if purchased whole and raw – if you want to use them ground or roasted it is best to prepare them yourself just before using them.

SOYA PRODUCE

Nowadays, wholefood shops and many supermarkets offer at least some of the products made from the high-protein, low-fat soya bean. If you are catering for a vegan, look out for soya milk and milk shakes, soya yogurt, soya mayonnaise, soya desserts, soya 'cream' and soya 'cheese'. You can also buy soya flour which, when added with water to wholemeal flour, can be used instead of eggs as a binding ingredient. And, of course, tofu (bean curd) and tempeh are widely available. Tofu is growing in popularity, and there are a number of recipes in this book showing you how to use it. Fresh tofu, whether plain, smoked or marinated, must be stored in a fridge and used within a short time, but you can also buy braised tofu (in cans) and dried tofu. Look out, too, for silken tofu, which is softer and therefore more suitable for desserts.

EGGS

Try not to use too many eggs, as they are high in cholesterol, and then only use free-range. Store them in a cool place, pointed ends down and well away from strongly flavoured foods.

DAIRY PRODUCTS

These are a valuable source of protein and other nutrients for vegetarians (not vegans – see page 9). Look out for cheeses labelled vegetarian – others are likely to have been made with animal rennet, which is taken from the stomach of calves. Some low-fat and soft cheeses are made without using rennet at all. Vegetarian Cheddar is widely available and some shops have recently started to stock a rennet-free Parmesan substitute. Do try some of the more unusual cheeses too, such as feta and mozzarella.

Yogurt is an excellent food and is now available in many varieties, bio-yogurt (which contains live culture) being the best. Avoid the ready-flavoured varieties which are usually full of sugar and may even contain gelatine. There are some excellent creams available (such as soured cream and crème fraîche) which, when added to savoury dishes, give a deliciously smooth texture. Butter has a much better flavour than margarine but is high in saturated fat (as are margarines unless they expressly state otherwise on the label), so use it in moderation.

DRIED FRUITS

Dried fruits are a natural food that is full of energy and infinitely preferable to manufactured sweets. Buy an assortment, choosing those that have not been sprayed or treated if possible. Store them in airtight containers, and get into the habit of adding them to all sorts of sweet and savoury dishes, even to salads. Great for school lunch boxes.

SAUCES AND FLAVOURINGS

These are always useful and come in many forms. Look out for sweet and sour sauces, piquant black or yellow bean sauces to use when stir-frying, and pesto sauce. Some that appear innocuous may contain forbidden ingredients – Worcestershire sauce, for example, is usually made with anchovies, though there is a vegetarian version. Check the labels, and when in doubt, don't buy without first checking with the manufacturers.

MEAT SUBSTITUTES

The best known type is TVP (Textured Vegetable Protein), a dehydrated product made from soya or other vegetable matter and available either 'beef' flavoured or plain, in chunks or mince. Simply add hot water or vegetable stock before using. TVP keeps well stored in its box in a cupboard. It is very nutritious, but it needs to be used in imaginative ways to add flavour.

CONVENIENCE FOODS

There are now plenty of vegetarian convenience foods, such as dry mixes that can be made into instant burgers, sausages and loaves. The same types of foods are available frozen, too, and you can also buy a range of ready-to-eat dishes and complete meals. Keep some frozen pastry – shortcrust, puff and filo – for when time is limited. Look out, too, for the growing selection of vegetable burgers and croquettes now being produced. These usually consist of finely chopped vegetables with either potato or rice to bind them, sometimes seeds or cheese added, and a crisp crumb coating. What makes them especially useful is that they can be served to vegetarians (perhaps with baked beans for extra protein), and also to non-vegetarians as an accompaniment to meat or fish dishes.

SUGAR AND SWEET SPREADS

All forms of sugar are acceptable to vegetarians, although vegans don't eat honey. Raw cane sugar contains a few nutrients, making it preferable to the more widely used refined white variety which is almost a pure chemical, with no nutritional value whatsoever. Other natural sweeteners include molasses, corn syrup, maple syrup and barley malt syrup – all of which are admittedly expensive, but a little goes a long way. However, for a healthy diet, all sugars should be reduced to a minimum for vegetarians and non-vegetarians alike.

Some final trouble-shooting tips

All too often it's the little things that flare up and cause problems. Here are some points to remember when there's a vegetarian in the family.

- Don't roast potatoes actually touching the meat, not if they're meant for everyone. Either keep them separate altogether, or cook a jacket potato for the vegetarian.
- Don't forget about the gravy! Again, the vegetarian will need one that doesn't contain meat fat or stock. It's probably worth making up a large amount of vegetarian gravy when you have time, freezing it in individual pots, then heating up one serving in a separate saucepan just before the meal is served. If both gravies have a similar colour, why not keep a special jug for the vegetarian version?
- You'll need separate serving spoons too.

- If you have vegetarian guests coming to dinner and you're unsure exactly what they eat, put everything out on the table, buffet-style, and invite everyone to help themselves. In fact, better still, ask beforehand if there's anything they don't eat..

- Don't feel that a meal has to be complicated to be enjoyable. There is nothing wrong with simple food – in fact, a simple meal prepared with love is infinitely better than the most wonderful spread prepared by someone who is tired and tense and resentful about being left to do all the work. Having to prepare food for vegetarians and non-vegetarians at the same time is demanding. Cut corners, cheat occasionally. A spoonful or two of yogurt can make just as tasty a topping as a homemade sauce. Frozen puff pastry gives wonderful results – and think of the time it saves. Bread warm from the oven need not actually have been kneaded by your own fair hands. A main dish can be served with salad and bread instead of potatoes and vegetables.

- There is a final point to be considered. Some vegetarians do find it difficult to sit and eat alongside someone who is breaking the legs off a lobster, winkling snails out of shells, or dabbing French bread into the pools of blood running off a piece of rare steak. If the vegetarian in your family feels this way, perhaps such meals should be kept for when the non-vegetarians are eating alone.

ANY QUESTIONS?

As with any new venture, taking up vegetarianism inevitably means there are lots of questions that you'll come across, some of them simple, others requiring more complex answers. Here are a selection of the ones I've been asked over the years.

Though I know a vegetarian diet is meant to be healthier, I'm worried that if I give up eating meat I'll be short of protein.

Nutritionists stress the value of restricting meat consumption, if not dropping it altogether. Vegetarians not only consume far fewer of the saturated fats implicated in heart disease (meat accounts for a high proportion of the total saturated fat intake for those who eat it), but they also tend to have lower blood cholesterol levels, a reduced incidence of cancer, are usually leaner – the list goes on. (This, of course, applies to those who not only give up eating flesh foods but replace them with wholefoods.)

Most western meat-based diets are in fact too high in protein, putting a strain on the digestive system which can cause still more health problems, especially for the overworked colon and kidneys. Having said that, you do, of course, need some protein each day. This will be amply supplied by nuts, seeds, grains and pulses (including soya products such as tofu, which are an especially rich source). Dairy products are also rich in protein. You won't need to use vast amounts of any of these – sprinkling a dish with nuts or cheese or stirring some tahini into a sauce will be plenty. Aim to vary your protein (and all) foods, combining them in ways that will boost the nutrients in a dish as well as making it more interesting to the taste buds.

All that pasta, potatoes and bread – they sound so fattening. Won't I put on weight?

Quite the opposite. The natural fibre in these foods will fill you up more quickly than refined foods, or, of course, those that contain no fibre at all such as meat, fish and dairy produce. (Vegetarians who eat wholemeal bread and pasta, brown rice, plus vegetables, fruit, pulses and nuts, consume twice as much fibre as the average meat eater.) So you'll also actually eat less, take in fewer calories, and cut your saturated fat consumption too.

It is best to avoid the many specially produced 'diet' foods, which are usually unnatural foods full of additives and may not be vegetarian. Some low-fat yogurts and low-fat butter substitutes, for example, contain gelatine. Aim instead to listen to your body – to eat only when you are hungry, and to leave the table before you are full. Try to eat just enough of the foods that keep your weight steady and your energy level high.

Once their bodies have adapted to the change, most people find they lose weight on a well-balanced vegetarian diet – though if you give up meat and replace it with doughnuts, salted peanuts and pot noodles, you may well have problems!

Since going to university my son has decided to become a vegan, and nothing I can say will change his mind. What on earth am I going to feed him when he comes home for the holiday?

Vegans are true vegetarians. They do not consume any products of animal origin, which means foods many vegetarians eat (dairy produce, eggs and honey, for example) are also avoided.

Though this may sound as though it leaves very little you can feed to the vegan in your family, don't despair. Apart from the many familiar products you can use – beans of all kinds, nuts, grains, vegetables and so son – there are now more and more vegan alternatives, both in wholefood shops and supermarkets. Look out for specially produced vegan cheeses, milk, yogurt, mayonnaise, ice-cream, and so on. Note, however, that some of these are produced to supply the growing demand for low-fat foods rather than for any ethical reasons, so do check the labels carefully. You'll also find a selection of ready-to-serve dishes.

Try, too, some of the vegan recipes given in this book – they are marked V+. Many more recipes can easily be adapted by using soya milk instead of dairy milk and soya flour instead of eggs when a binding ingredient is needed. Cuisines from around the world are often rich in vegan dishes, Indian food being especially suitable.

Having a sensitive stomach, I have to admit that although I enjoy vegetarian food very much I often find it hard to digest. Any tips?

This is a familiar problem, especially for anyone new to vegetarianism. After years of a low-fibre, high-protein diet, it's obvious your digestive system is going to have to make some adjustments. It is for this reason that a gradual changeover is wiser than making the switch overnight. Some people simply reduce the number of meat or fish dishes they eat, replacing them with grains and vegetables and allowing their stomach to get used to the increased fibre gradually. Many people nowadays call themselves demi-vegetarians, which means they have dropped red meat from their diet and eat just chicken and fish plus vegetarian dishes. This, too, is an excellent way to ease yourself into being completely vegetarian.

However, there are some other things you can do to help. Pulses are almost certainly the main problem. If these cause flatulence, it may be that you are not cooking them properly. Soak them for about eight hours, then drain and cover them with fresh water before cooking. Make sure they are completely cooked – this can take hours, but don't be tempted to skimp. If you eat beans often, cook up extra and freeze them, or use a pressure cooker. If time is really limited, use canned beans.

Don't be tempted to serve pulses in huge amounts – a plateful of beans is likely to give anyone a stomach ache! Traditionally they are often combined with grains, in dishes such as chilli beans and tacos, lentil curry and rice. A spoonful or two of yogurt, either dairy or soya, also goes very well with bean dishes, as do spices such as ginger and fennel, and herbs such as mint – all useful aids to digestion. As the nutritional benefits of beans are not lost if you grind or mash them, try eating them in the form of bean burgers, hummus or bean pâté, and you may well find that the problem disappears. And do use tofu frequently – soya beans at their most digestible!

I'm planning a barbecue and now discover that three of my guests are vegetarian. Is there anything special I can do for them, or are they going to have to make do with jacket potatoes?

So that they don't stand out from everyone else – not all vegetarians welcome the opportunity to be the centre of attention – try to match the vegetarian fare to the rest. For example, if you're cooking burgers, cook vegetarian burgers too, and serve them with baps, barbecue sauce and relishes. Kebabs are a barbecue favourite, and it's easy to make a vegetarian version using all sorts of ingredients – tofu, canned or frozen meatless sausages cut into chunks, marinated TVP chunks, plus vegetables such as onions, peppers, fennel, courgettes, cherry tomatoes and mushrooms. Cook them in the same way as you would meat kebabs, brushing them first with oil and turning them frequently so that they don't burn.

Corn on the cob can be cooked in the husks – simply turn them back, pull out the silks and brush the corn itself with oil, then tie the husks in place again and put them on to the barbecue. Whole onions can be cooked in the same way, as can peppers, beef tomatoes, and, of course, potatoes. Alternatively, you could make vegetable parcels: mix some chopped vegetables together and add herb butter, grated cheese or nuts. Stir in a few spoonfuls of cooked rice or bulgur wheat, if you like. Wrap the filling carefully in double-thickness squares of silver foil, seal the edges and place on the barbecue.

Salads, breads, and a selection of desserts can be served to vegetarians and non-vegetarians alike.

We don't have a wholefood shop nearby, so have to use a supermarket. Though you say most supermarkets now cater for vegetarians, how can I be sure a product that looks suitable really is?

This is a very real problem for vegetarians, and can result in you having to spend hours studying labels and then trying to make sense of what you read.

There are, of course, a number of foods that are obviously suitable. Canned or dried beans, free-range eggs, tofu, rice . . . all these are familiar items and will be clearly labelled.

Many convenience foods such as sauces, soups, dressings, ready-to-eat meals, plus a whole range of desserts can also be perfectly fine for vegetarians. Some, however, are most definitely not. Yogurt may contain gelatine, a gâteau may contain shellac, a tomato sauce may be flavoured with chicken stock, a quiche made with factory-farmed eggs and non-vegetarian cheese, and cakes may be made with animal fats. Although these details will be listed on the label, they may well be disguised under a generic term such as 'emulsifier', or even vaguer E numbers.

There are two things you can do. One is to choose products flashed as being suitable for vegetarians, either on the shelf or on the product itself. A number of supermarkets and stores are using this technique to draw the attention of interested customers. Look out, too, for The Vegetarian Society's green V symbol.

The second thing to do is to ask, either in person or by letter. Bring it home to stores and food manufacturers that vegetarians are making up a large proportion of the buying public – i.e. their customers! – and have a right to know what foods contain. Hopefully, such pressure will also persuade manufacturers to substitute ingredients acceptable to everyone whenever possible.

It's all very well saying you'll find everything you want in your local healthfood shops – but have you seen the prices they charge?

This is another familiar complaint, and it's easy to understand how someone new to vegetarianism might have a shock the first time they go shopping. Certainly some of the imported products and ready-to-eat meals are expensive – these are luxury items for those who can afford them. But even for those who can't there are plenty of good buys to be found.

Because wholefoods offer considerably better food value than junk foods, you'll need to use less of them. For example, sesame seeds are a wonderful ingredient full of nutrients, especially calcium – weight for weight they contain ten times as much as milk. You only need to sprinkle a small amount of them over a dish to give it a deliciously crunchy texture *and* to boost the nutrients. Using rich foods such as these as supplements or garnishes makes both nutritional and economic sense.

Base your meals on the less expensive ingredients such as pulses, grains and vegetables. That doesn't have to mean eating plates of rice every day! Look at the recipes for Tofu Moussaka (page 106), Mixed Vegetable Curry with Coconut Sauce (page 144), Hazelnut Pancakes Peperonata (page 162) – all these are based on less expensive ingredients, yet none can be called boring!

Though you might need to go to speciality shops for some ingredients, do also keep an eye on your local supermarket shelves. As interest in healthy eating grows, so does the range of items supermarkets offer, and because they sell in bulk their prices are often considerably lower.

Though I live alone and therefore don't have to fit in with others, I'm also out at work all day and often arrive home too tired to want to cook. Have you any suggestions?

There are certainly foods that are especially quick and easy to cook. Pasta is an obvious choice. You could also stock up on bulgur wheat (cracked wheat that can be prepared in minutes) and quick-cooking brown rice. For sauces or toppings keep in a supply of such items as pesto sauce, mixed Italian-style vegetables and olives. Frozen vegetable dishes such as ratatouille are also useful – mix them with some beans (from a can if necessary), then serve with a grain and some salad.

Other easy meals include anything made with eggs, stir-fries and most tofu dishes. Invest in a good-quality wok if you haven't already – an excellent aid to saving not just time but also nutrients.

If you do sometimes have an hour or two spare, why not make up some sauces and freeze them in individual containers? You could do the same with cooked beans, pancakes and grains, plus, of course, many of the dishes in this book. You will then have instant meals you can heat in the oven or microwave when you arrive home.

My daughter is twelve years old and a vegetarian. Though I know this way of eating is healthy for adults, she is still growing, and I'm concerned that she may regret her decision in later years. How can I persuade her to eat meat at least occasionally?

Statistics show that of the many children becoming vegetarian the largest proportion is those aged between eleven and eighteen years. Not only can a balanced vegetarian diet provide all the nutrients their bodies need, but there is also increasing evidence to show that there are added benefits to growing up vegetarian. Lower cholesterol levels, stronger bones, less tendency to put on weight are just some of the pluses that your daughter may well benefit from in later life.

The key words, of course, are 'balanced diet', but even this is easier to achieve than it might sound. Firstly – if she hasn't already done this for herself – encourage her to eat fewer junk foods. Refined foods full of additives and sugar aren't good for anyone. In fact, they're hardly 'foods' at all. Replace them with wholefoods, varying these as much as possible and experimenting with ingredients you might not have tried before. Make sure that each day she has some protein (from beans, tofu, grains, nuts, seeds, eggs and low-fat dairy produce), some vegetables and fruit. A raw salad a day is also a good policy. For anyone who claims to hate salad, try sandwiching it between two slices of fresh wholemeal bread spread with nut butter, hummus or low-fat cheese – and watch it disappear.

Rather than worrying about exact amounts, just make a point of having fun with recipes, and encourage your daughter to help you prepare them or even to cook something herself. And rather than trying to persuade her to eat meat occasionally – which she most certainly doesn't need – how about joining her in eating a vegetarian meal?

With so many members of our family turning vegetarian, Christmas get-togethers are becoming a nightmare! Is there anything I can do to cut corners?

The family get-together, enjoyable though it may be, is never easy for the cook, but there are several things you can do to make it less difficult.

Do try to make as many dishes as possible suitable for everyone, vegetarians and non-vegetarians alike. If you make your own Christmas pudding and mincemeat, consider making only vegetarian versions (e.g. using vegetable suet), which require only simple adaptations, no extra expense, and will be enjoyed by everyone. If you think the traditionalists in the family won't approve, don't tell them – they are unlikely to notice the difference.

Everyone can eat the vegetables you plan to serve, as long as you don't don't use meat stock for cooking, and don't cook the potatoes alongside the meat. The stuffing you serve with the turkey can also be made from wholesome, animal-free ingredients, cooked separately from the bird, and served to the vegetarians.

The turkey is, of course, the one dish you're going to have to replace completely. A nut roast of some kind is a popular choice as it can be cooked in the oven with the turkey (make sure it is covered with foil so that it doesn't absorb the flavour) and will usually go well with cranberry sauce (see page 120). Make your roast as simple or exotic as you like – anything from peanut loaf to one made with pine nuts, curry paste and aubergine. Alternatively, how about wrapping puff pastry around vegetables in a cream sauce, and shaping it into a Christmas cracker? Or making a Brussels sprout and chestnut strudel? Or using the stuffing to fill a selection of vegetables such as peppers, tomatoes and fennel, and sprinkling them with Parmesan cheese?

If you have a freezer, do make use of it. Unlike the turkey, many vegetarian dishes can be prepared weeks in advance and frozen, saving you time, energy and kitchen space on Christmas day.

BREAKFASTS

Apart from the traditional fry-up, few breakfast dishes are meat based, but it's still a good idea to stop and consider exactly what both the vegetarian in the family and everyone else eat each morning.

Your breakfast sets you up for the day. After at least eight hours of fasting (probably the longest period most of us go without food), you need something more than a puff of refined wheat sprinkled with white sugar and drenched with milk. You need food supercharged with quality carbohydrates, protein, vitamins and minerals.

This doesn't mean you have to eat a huge meal – far from it. In fact, as your stomach has shrunk during the night you may well find it difficult to eat much at all. This is why it's especially important to eat a wholefood breakfast. If cereal is all you can face, make sure it's made from whole grains, and add some nuts, dried fruit, and maybe some fresh fruit. If you can only manage a slice of toast, use wholemeal bread and add a yeast or nut spread or, if it has to be something sweet, how about banana mashed with honey?

If a more substantial breakfast appeals, there are plenty of alternatives for both the vegetarian and vegan. Eggs, a traditional favourite at this time of day, are fine if they are free range. You could even serve a vegetarian version of the traditional fry up (see page 46).

Barley Malt Granola

V+

Granola is a crunchy, cooked version of muesli. You can vary the ingredients to suit your own personal taste – and what's in the cupboard. Serve for breakfast with milk (soya milk for vegans), or sprinkle it over puréed fruit, ice-cream or yogurt. Perfect for just nibbling when you need instant energy!

Preparation time: 10 minutes
Cooking time: 20 minutes

METRIC/IMPERIAL	AMERICAN
·4 tablespoons vegetable oil	4 tablespoons vegetable oil
4–6 tablespoons barley malt syrup	4–6 tablespoons barley malt syrup
2 tablespoons grated orange rind	2 tablespoons grated orange rind
680g/1½ lb mixed cereal base	6 cups mixed cereal base
55g/2 oz almonds, chopped	½ cup chopped almonds
55g/2 oz cashew pieces	½ cup cashew pieces
55g/2 oz sesame seeds	½ cup sesame seeds
85g/3 oz desiccated coconut	1 cup shredded coconut
170g/6 oz raisins	1 cup raisins

1 In a saucepan gently heat the oil and barley malt syrup (using more syrup if you have a sweeter tooth), stirring frequently until well blended. Add the orange rind.

2 Stir in the cereal base, almonds, cashews, sesame seeds and coconut. Spread the mixture on to one or two baking trays.

3 Bake in the oven at 180°C/350°F (Gas Mark 4) for about 20 minutes, stirring occasionally. The granola is ready when lightly browned and crisp – the longer you cook it, the richer it will taste.

4 Turn off the heat, stir in the raisins, and leave in the oven to cool, with the oven door slightly open. Store in an airtight container and use as needed.

TIP Barley malt syrup gives this granola a distinctive taste. You can replace it with maple syrup or honey, if you eat it.

Scrambled Tofu on Toast

V+

Try this as an unusual vegan alternative to scrambled eggs. For a more filling dish, add lightly cooked vegetables such as onion, tomatoes, mushrooms or peas. It makes a good topping for jacket potatoes too, or a filling for pancakes.

Preparation time: 5 minutes (plus draining the tofu)
Cooking time: 10 minutes

METRIC/IMPERIAL	AMERICAN
285g/10 oz tofu	1¼ cups tofu
2 tablespoons vegetable oil	2 tablespoons vegetable oil
¼ teaspoon turmeric	¼ teaspoon turmeric
¼ teaspoon garlic salt	¼ teaspoon garlic salt
1 teaspoon dried mixed herbs	1 teaspoon dried mixed herbs
4 slices wholemeal bread	4 slices wholewheat bread
margarine	margarine
2 tomatoes, cut into quarters	2 tomatoes, cut into quarters
fresh parsley sprigs	fresh parsley sprigs

1 Drain the tofu well to remove all moisture. (The easiest way to do this is to wrap it in a clean tea towel, put a weight on top, and leave for at least 10 minutes, preferably longer.) Use a fork to mash the tofu coarsely.
2 Heat the oil in a saucepan then add the tofu, turmeric, garlic salt and herbs. Cook gently, stirring continually, until heated through.
3 Meanwhile toast the bread, spread with margarine, and put on to 4 plates. Divide the mixture between the slices, decorate with the tomato quarters and parsley sprigs and serve at once.

TIP Instead of turmeric, use garam masala and omit the herbs. Smoked tofu has a more distinctive flavour than plain – use it for a change.

Cheesy Oatmeal Pancakes

These small pancakes have an interesting texture. Serve them just as they are, or with tomatoes, mushrooms or scrambled eggs. If you prefer, omit the mustard and cheese and top with sliced bananas and maybe a drizzle of honey or syrup.

Preparation time: 5 minutes
Cooking time: 10 minutes

METRIC/IMPERIAL	AMERICAN
55g/2 oz oatmeal	½ cup oatmeal
55g/2 oz wholemeal flour	½ cup wholewheat flour
1 tablespoon baking powder	1 tablespoon baking powder
½ teaspoon dry mustard	½ teaspoon dry mustard
pinch of salt	pinch of salt
1 large free-range egg, beaten	1 large free-range egg, beaten
55g/2 oz Cheddar cheese, grated	½ cup grated Cheddar cheese
400ml/⅔ pint milk and water, mixed	1½ cups milk and water
vegetable oil for frying	vegetable oil for frying

1 Mix together the oatmeal, flour, baking powder, mustard and ·
   salt. (For smoother-textured pancakes, grind the oatmeal first.)
2 Gradually mix in the egg, cheese and milk and water. The batter
   should be smooth but not too thick.
3 Heat a little oil in a small frying pan, drop in a few spoonfuls
   of the batter, and tilt the pan so the mixture covers the base.
   Cook gently until crisp and brown underneath. Flip the
   pancake or turn it with a spatula, cook the other side, then serve
   at once (or keep it warm while using up the rest of the mixture
   in the same way, then serve everyone at the same time).

*TIP Save time in the morning by making up the batter the night before and
leaving it in the fridge. Whisk lightly again in the morning before using,
adding a drop more liquid if it seems too thick.*

Banana Wheatgerm Muesli

V+

This makes enough muesli to supply one person for a week. Add milk (soya milk for vegans) before eating. For a thicker, smoother muesli soak a few spoonfuls per person in cold water overnight (if using this method, add the banana chips separately in the morning).

Preparation time: 5 minutes
Cooking time: None

METRIC/IMPERIAL	AMERICAN
455g/1 lb oatflakes	4 cups oatflakes
55g/2 oz toasted wheatgerm	½ cup toasted wheatgerm
55g/2 oz light raw cane sugar	⅓ cup light raw cane sugar
115g/4 oz hazelnuts, whole or coarsely chopped	¾ cup hazelnuts, whole or coarsely chopped
115g/4 oz sunflower seeds	1 cup sunflower seeds
115g/4 oz banana chips	1 cup banana chips

1 In a large bowl mix together the oatflakes, wheatgerm, sugar, hazelnuts and sunflower seeds. The banana chips can be added straight away or put on the table in a separate bowl to be sprinkled over the top.
2 Store the mix in an airtight container and use as needed.

TIP You can buy raw wheatgerm and toast it yourself, or look out for ready toasted wheatgerm. (If you prefer, use it raw). Any mixture of grains can be used in muesli, and any nuts, seeds and dried fruits can be added. Fresh fruit can be added at the table. This muesli is also good added to flapjacks, or to the topping when making fruit crumble.

Tempeh Sandwiches

———◆•◆———

V+

The perfect breakfast for any vegan who misses their fried bacon sandwiches! If time is limited, you can now buy tempeh 'rashers' all ready for frying – check your local wholefood shop.

Preparation time: 5 minutes
Cooking time: 10 minutes

METRIC/IMPERIAL
225g/8 oz tempeh (see Tip below)

soy sauce to taste

vegetable oil for frying

8 slices wholemeal bread

vegan margarine

AMERICAN
1 cup tempeh (see Tip below)

soy sauce to taste

vegetable oil for frying

8 slices wholewheat bread

vegan margarine

1 With a sharp knife, cut the tempeh into very thin strips, then sprinkle lightly with soy sauce.
2 Heat the oil in a frying pan and fry the strips, turning occasionally, until crisp.
3 Spread the bread with the margarine, divide the tempeh between 4 slices, then top each one with another slice. Serve immediately.

TIP Tempeh is a fermented soya bean curd with a slightly chewy texture and strong flavour. It is usually available frozen, and though it should be defrosted before using, it is easier to cut it into thin slices while it is still very cold. Marinate it for a while in soy sauce (maybe adding garlic) for even more flavour.

Sunflower Waffles with Apple Purée

To make these waffles extra nutritious, soya flour is added to them with the sunflower seeds. If you don't have any soya flour you could use oatmeal instead.

Preparation time: 20 minutes
Cooking time: 25 minutes

METRIC/IMPERIAL	AMERICAN
115g/4 oz wholemeal flour	1 cup wholewheat flour
30g/1 oz soya flour	¼ cup soy flour
1 tablespoon baking powder	1 tablespoon baking powder
1 teaspoon mixed spice	1 teaspoon mixed spice
2 free-range eggs, separated	2 free-range eggs, separated
285ml/½ pint milk	1¼ cups milk
55g/2 oz margarine, melted	¼ cup margarine, melted
30g/1 oz raw cane sugar	2 tablespoons raw cane sugar
85g/3 oz sunflower seeds	¾ cup sunflower seeds

For the apple purée
For the apple purée

455g/1 lb cooking apples, peeled, cored and sliced	1 pound cooking apples, peeled, cored and sliced
1 tablespoon chopped lemon rind	1 tablespoon chopped lemon rind
½ teaspoon ground cinnamon	½ teaspoon ground cinnamon
¼ teaspoon ground cloves	¼ teaspoon ground cloves
55g/2 oz raw cane sugar	⅓ cup raw cane sugar

1 Put the apples into a saucepan with the lemon rind, spices and sugar. Cover and cook gently until the apples collapse, adding a drop of water if necessary (do not add too much – the purée should be fairly dry). Sieve or mash until fairly smooth.
2 Sift together the flours, baking powder and mixed spice. In a separate bowl lightly beat the egg yolks, then add the milk, melted margarine and sugar.
3 Make a well in the centre of the dry ingredients and gradually stir in the liquid. If the batter seems dry, add a drop more milk.
4 Whisk the egg whites until just beginning to stiffen, then use a metal spoon to fold them into the batter, adding the sunflower seeds at the same time.
5 Grease a waffle iron, heat for a few minutes, then pour in just enough batter to cover it. Close the iron and leave for 2 minutes – the waffle should be crisp and golden. Serve at once, with hot or cold apple purée, using the rest of the batter in the same way.

TIP Most good kitchen shops carry a selection of waffle irons. Make sure you grease the iron between each batch. Waffles are ideal not just for breakfast but for lunch and late-night snacks, too, and can be topped with a variety of savoury or sweet ingredients.

Mushroom-topped French Toast

This is a good dish for when you have time to linger and enjoy breakfast – though it takes less time to prepare than you may think. French toast is usually eaten with syrup or honey, but this savoury version is kinder to your teeth.

Preparation time: 10 minutes
Cooking time: 10 minutes

METRIC/IMPERIAL	AMERICAN
170g/6 oz button mushrooms	3 cups button mushrooms
55g/2 oz margarine	¼ cup margarine
30g/1 oz walnuts, coarsely chopped	2 tablespoons coarsely chopped walnuts
2 tablespoons milk	2 tablespoons milk
2 free-range eggs	2 free-range eggs
seasoning to taste	seasoning to taste
6 slices wholemeal bread	6 slices wholewheat bread
vegetable oil for frying	vegetable oil for frying
chopped fresh chives	chopped fresh chives

1 Wipe clean the mushrooms then cut them into thick slices. Melt the margarine and fry the mushrooms until just cooked, then add the walnuts and cook a minute or so longer. Remove from the heat but keep the mixture warm.
2 In a shallow dish, beat together the milk, eggs and seasoning.
3 Trim the crusts from the bread and cut each slice across into triangles.
4 Heat the oil in a frying pan. Dip the bread into the egg mixture, fry for a minute, then turn and fry the other side.
5 Put three triangles of toast on each plate, top with some of the mushroom mixture and sprinkle with chopped chives. Serve at once.

TIP A vegan version of French toast can be made by whisking together ground cashew nuts and soya milk, then dipping the bread triangles into the mixture and frying as described above.

Dried Fruit Compote with Tahini Cream

V+

Here that old favourite, stewed prunes, is given a new twist. Dried fruit is rich in iron, which is especially important for anyone no longer eating meat. Add tahini cream and you've got a dish full of nutrients, ideal for anyone who hates eating breakfast.

Preparation time: 5 minutes (plus soaking overnight)
Cooking time: A few minutes

METRIC/IMPERIAL	AMERICAN
115g/4 oz dried apricots	1 cup dried apricots
115g/4 oz dried pears	1 cup dried pears
115g/4 oz prunes	1 cup prunes
115g/4 oz raisins	⅔ cup raisins
425ml/¾ pint China tea	2 cups China tea
70ml/2½ fl oz orange juice	¼ cup orange juice
1 tablespoon grated lemon rind	1 tablespoon grated lemon rind
115g/4 oz silken tofu	½ cup silken tofu
4 tablespoons light tahini	4 tablespoons light tahini
2 tablespoons concentrated apple juice, or to taste	2 tablespoons concentrated apple juice, or to taste

1 Put the fruit into a saucepan. Make the tea (do not, of course, add milk) and pour this over the fruit. Add the orange juice and lemon rind.
2 Bring to a boil, cover and simmer for a few minutes, then turn off the heat and leave the fruit to soak overnight.
3 To make the tahini cream, combine the drained tofu with the tahini and the apple juice in a blender. Adjust the consistency and sweetness to taste.
4 Serve the fruit in small bowls with a spoonful or two of tahini cream on top.

TIP For a sharper taste, add slices of fresh grapefruit to the dried fruit. You can use syrup or honey instead of the apple juice. This dish also makes a delicious dessert.

Vegetarian Fried Breakfast

Basically the same as the non-vegetarians in the family are having, but with a few substitutions – and as quantities are for four, why not get everyone to try it?

Preparation time: 5 minutes
Cooking time: 10–15 minutes

METRIC/IMPERIAL	AMERICAN
395g/14 oz can vegetarian sausages	medium can vegetarian sausages
115g/4 oz mushrooms	2 cups mushrooms
6 tomatoes	6 tomatoes
vegetable oil for frying	vegetable oil for frying
4 slices wholemeal bread	4 slices wholewheat bread
4 free-range eggs	4 free-range eggs
395g/14 oz can baked beans	medium can baked beans
sauces to serve	sauces to serve

1 Drain the sausages and pat dry. Clean and slice the mushrooms. Halve the tomatoes.
2 Heat a small amount of oil in a heavy-based frying pan and gently fry the sausages, turning them frequently, until brown. Then drain and keep them warm.
3 Add a little more oil and fry the mushrooms and tomatoes. When cooked, remove them from the pan. Cut the bread into triangles and fry briefly until crisp and brown on both sides, then drain well.
4 Fry the eggs last, and heat the baked beans in a separate pan.
5 Divide the ingredients between 4 warmed plates and serve with a selection of sauces.

TIP Vegetarian sausages are also available either freshly made (look in the chiller cabinet in your local wholefood shop) or frozen. You can also make them up from a dry mix – Sosmix could almost be the real thing, without gristle. This is also a good opportunity to use up leftovers such as potatoes (make potato cakes), cabbage (fried) and nut loaf (cut into fingers and fried).

Bran Muffins

V+

If you don't like cereals, here's another way of getting your daily bran. Warm from the oven, sweet and crumbly, they're a very nice way to start your day. This is a vegan version.

Preparation time: 10 minutes
Cooking time: 20 minutes

METRIC/IMPERIAL	AMERICAN
170g/6 oz wholemeal flour	1½ cups wholewheat flour
1 tablespoon baking powder	1 tablespoon bakinig powder
55g/2 oz bran	½ cup bran
15g/½ oz vegan margarine	1 tablespoon vegan margarine
200ml/⅓ pint soya milk	¾ cup soy milk
1 tablespoon syrup	1 tablespoon syrup
85g/3 oz raw cane sugar	½ cup raw cane sugar

1 Sift together the flour, baking powder and bran.
2 Melt the margarine in a small saucepan, add the milk and syrup and heat gently, stirring continually. When the mixture is well blended, mix quickly into the dry ingredients. Stir in the sugar.
3 The batter should be fairly wet – add more milk if necessary. Then divide between 8 lightly greased muffin tins, filling them not quite to the top.
4 Bake in the oven at 200°C/400°F (Gas Mark 6) for about 20 minutes or until risen. Turn out of the tin on to a rack to cool. Serve with margarine and jam or marmalade.

TIP Vegetarians can replace the syrup with an egg and use dairy milk instead of soya. Dried fruit and/or nuts can also be added. Although wheat bran is the most widely known type, do also experiment with different kinds such as oat and rice bran.

SNACKS AND STARTERS

It wasn't so long ago that we were told snacks were bad for us. Now, though, it is generally believed that eating small amounts often is easier on the digestive system. Because we use up the calories as we go along rather than storing them, snacking can help us to stay slim. And by constantly topping up we keep our energy levels high, making it easier to get through the day.

Of course, everyone's idea of a snack will differ. For one it may be a chocolate bar eaten while driving from A to B, for another a bag of chips, for another a piece of fruit with yogurt. And for the outdoor worker, it may well be all three!

Even though snacks might now have the go-ahead, it's important – not just for vegetarians, but for everyone – to avoid junk foods. Replace them with snacks based on ingredients that are as natural and wholesome as possible. Not only is there a wide and ever-expanding choice available these days, but if time allows you can also make your own healthier versions of the most popular snacks – and probably for half the price.

The recipes that follow are, on the whole, quick and easy to prepare. They're also very versatile in that they can be served in a variety of ways. They make perfect snacks to be consumed at lunchtime, out in the garden or in front of the TV, but many of them can also be dished up as first courses for dinner. In this case, do pay attention to the dishes you serve them in and be imaginative with the garnishes.

Aubergine (Eggplant) and Hazelnut Pâté with Melba Toast

V+

Based on a Middle Eastern dish, this unusual pâté isn't difficult to make, and can be varied in all sorts of ways – for example, use almonds instead of hazelnuts, or tahini. For parties, or as a starter, use the pâté to stuff mushrooms and heat briefly. It also makes an exotic sandwich filling.

Preparation time: 15 minutes
Cooking time: 45 minutes

METRIC/IMPERIAL	AMERICAN
2 small aubergines	2 small eggplants
1 clove garlic, crushed	1 clove garlic, crushed
2 tablespoons olive oil, plus a little extra for baking aubergines	2 tablespoons olive oil, plus a little extra for baking eggplants
2 tablespoons lemon juice	2 tablespoons lemon juice
¼ teaspoon paprika, or to taste	¼ teaspoon paprika, or to taste
55g/2 oz hazelnuts, preferably roasted	½ cup hazelnuts, preferably roasted
black olives and chopped fresh parsley to garnish	black olives and chopped fresh parsley to garnish
Melba toast to serve (see Tip below)	Melba toast to serve (see Tip below)

1 Rub the aubergines (eggplants) with a little olive oil, place them on a baking tray, and bake in the oven at 180°C/350°F (Gas Mark 4) for about 45 minutes, or until soft when pressed.

2 Grasp each aubergine (eggplant) by the stalk, and hold under a cold tap while stripping off the skin. (Though this is a simple and efficient way to peel them you can, if you prefer, halve them then use a spoon to scoop out the flesh.)

3 Chop the aubergine (eggplant) flesh and purée it in a blender with the garlic, olive oil, lemon juice and paprika. When smooth transfer it to a bowl. Grind the nuts to a powder and stir into the aubergine mixture. The resulting pâté should be thick and smooth – add more nuts if necessary.

4 Turn the mixture into a small bowl and, if time allows, cover and chill briefly. Sprinkle with olives and parsley before serving with Melba toast.

TIP To make Melba toast, lightly toast 4 slices of bread, cut them in half then, using a very sharp knife, carefully cut through each slice to make even thinner slices. Cut into fingers or triangles. Use a grill (broiler) to toast the uncooked side until it begins to curl. Melba toast can be served warm, or cooled and stored in an airtight container for use later.

Avocado and Pink Grapefruit Salad

V+

This makes a refreshing snack on a hot summer's day, especially if served on a base of crisp lettuce leaves and accompanied by wholemeal rolls. It can also be served in the grapefruit skins as a starter.

Preparation time: 10 minutes
Cooking time: 5 minutes

METRIC/IMPERIAL	AMERICAN
55g/2 oz flaked almonds	½ cup flaked almonds
2 large ripe avocados	2 large ripe avocados
2 pink grapefruit	2 pink grapefruit
4 tablespoons vegetable oil	4 tablespoons vegetable oil
2 tablespoons cider vinegar	2 tablespoons cider vinegar
1 teaspoon finely chopped fresh mint	1 teaspoon finely chopped fresh mint
seasoning to taste	seasoning to taste

1 Dry-roast the almonds by spreading them out in a heavy-based saucepan and cooking them over a medium heat, stirring frequently, until lightly browned. Set aside.
2 Halve, stone and peel the avocados, then cut them into thin slices and arrange on 4 small plates.
3 Peel the grapefruit and divide into segments. Make an overlapping circle of these on top of the avocado slices.
4 Beat together the oil, vinegar, mint and seasoning to make a dressing. Shake well, then pour a little over each plate. Sprinkle with the almonds and serve at once.

TIP *A more unusual salad dressing for this recipe can be made by mixing together 2 tablespoons of a light oil such as sunflower and 4 tablespoons grapefruit juice.*

Blue Cheese Pâté Roll

Serve this highly flavoured pâté with French bread and celery for lunch, or accompanied with fruit such as grapes and sliced apple for an unusual finish to a special meal.

Preparation time: 10 minutes (plus chilling)
Cooking time: None

METRIC/IMPERIAL	AMERICAN
115g/4 oz blue cheese	½ cup blue cheese
115g/4 oz ricotta or curd cheese	½ cup ricotta or curd cheese
1–2 teaspoons milk (optional)	1–2 teaspoons milk (optional)
seasoning to taste	seasoning to taste
1 packet plain potato crisps	1 packet plain potato chips
watercress and radishes to garnish	watercress and radishes to garnish
wholemeal crackers to serve	wholewheat crackers to serve

1 Crumble the blue cheese into a bowl. Use a fork to mash it together with the ricotta or curd cheese.
2 The mixture should be quite firm, but if it seems too stiff, add a little milk. Season well.
3 Use your hands to shape the mixture into a roll. Coarsely crush the potato crisps (potato chips) and roll the cheese in them to make a crisp coating. Wrap it in silver foil and chill for 1 hour.
4 Cut the pâté into thin slices, garnish with radishes and watercress and serve with crackers.

TIP Make double the quantity, divide into 2 rolls and freeze one. Coarsely crushed walnuts or crushed black peppercorns could be used to coat the cheese.

Potato Scotch Eggs

Favourite picnic and lunch box fare, Scotch eggs can be made from a variety of ingredients. This particularly inexpensive version uses potato for a creamy coating that's also quite substantial. Just add salad for a summer lunch that everyone will enjoy.

Preparation time: 20 minutes
Cooking time: 20 minutes

METRIC/IMPERIAL	AMERICAN
1 potato, peeled and diced	1 potato, peeled and diced
1 small onion, finely chopped	1 small onion, finely chopped
1 carrot, finely grated	1 carrot, finely grated
115g/4 oz mixed nuts, grated	¾ cup grated mixed nuts
½ teaspoon dried marjoram	½ teaspoon dried marjoram
½ teaspoon dried thyme	½ teaspoon dried thyme
2 tablespoons tomato paste	2 tablespoons tomato paste
garlic salt	garlic salt
freshly ground black pepper	freshly ground black pepper
4 free-range eggs	4 free-range eggs
1 large free-range egg, beaten	1 large free-range egg, beaten
115g/4 oz dried wholemeal breadcrumbs	1 cup dried wholewheat breadcrumbs
vegetable oil for deep-frying	vegetable oil for deep-frying

1 Steam the potato cubes until soft. Drain well, mash to a smooth purée, then combine with the onion, carrot, nuts, herbs, tomato paste and seasoning to taste. The resulting mixture should be thick and smooth. If you like, add just a little of the beaten egg to help bind the mixture.

2 Lower the eggs into boiling water and boil them for 8 minutes. When cool, shell the hard-boiled eggs and pat dry. Divide the potato mixture into 4, then use your hands to mould it around each of the eggs, making sure the coating is even and smoothing the surface.

3 Dip each coated egg into the beaten egg, then into the breadcrumbs. Deep-fry them in hot oil until crisp and golden. Drain well and set aside to cool. Serve halved or quartered with salad and fresh bread.

TIP Vary the potato mix by using different herbs and/or nuts. Or try something completely different such as mashed cooked beans mixed with lightly cooked mushrooms and leeks, adding soy sauce for extra flavour. Or use cooked rice bound with an egg. There are also numerous vegetarian sausage and burger mixes that make excellent Scotch eggs. For a vegan version, fill the centre with mashed tofu mixed with seeds and herbs.

Tofu Fingers

Serve these in place of fish fingers – even the fish fanciers in the family may well enjoy them. Or dish them up garnished with lemon wedges, watercress and Hollandaise sauce as the first course at a dinner party.

Preparation time: 5 minutes
Cooking time: 10 minutes

METRIC/IMPERIAL	AMERICAN
340g/12 oz smoked tofu	1½ cups smoked tofu
55g/2 oz wholemeal flour	½ cup wholewheat flour
1 free-range egg, beaten	1 free-range egg, beaten
85g/3 oz wholemeal breadcrumbs	1½ cups wholewheat breadcrumbs
vegetable oil for frying	vegetable oil for frying

1 Drain the tofu well and pat dry. Cut into 8 even-sized fingers.
2 Dip the fingers into the flour, then the beaten egg, then the breadcrumbs, making sure they are thickly and evenly coated on all sides.
3 Heat some vegetable oil in a frying pan and fry the fingers for just a few minutes, or until the coating is crisp and golden. Drain them and serve at once. Good for a quick family lunch with new potatoes and salad.

TIP Use plain tofu if you prefer. Vegans can make a paste of flour and water instead of using an egg, then proceed as described above.

Curried Egg and Celery Salad

———— • ◆ • ————

Much more interesting than egg mayonnaise! Though the recipe suggests serving it on a plate, it's also delicious stuffed into warm pita bread.

Preparation time: 10 minutes
Cooking time: 8 minutes

METRIC/IMPERIAL	AMERICAN
4 large free-range eggs	4 large free-range eggs
2 sticks celery, chopped	2 sticks celery, chopped
1 red pepper, sliced	1 red pepper, sliced
6 tablespoons fromage frais	6 tablespoons fromage frais
1–2 teaspoons curry paste, or to taste	1–2 teaspoons curry paste, or to taste
1 small head endive lettuce	1 small head chicory
30g/1 oz coconut flakes, lightly toasted	⅓ cup coconut flakes, lightly toasted

1 Lower the eggs into boiling water and boil them for 8 minutes. Cool them, then shell and chop coarsely.
2 In a bowl, stir together the eggs, celery and red pepper.
3 Mix together the fromage frais and curry paste, adjusting the amount of curry to taste, then carefully combine with the egg mixture. Serve the salad on a bed of endive lettuce (chicory), sprinkled with coconut flakes.

TIP You can use soured cream, yogurt or mayonnaise instead of the fromage frais. If coconut flakes seem too strange a garnish, replace them with fresh parsley.

Summer Bulgur Salad

V+

Quick-to-prepare bulgur – or cracked wheat – is a favourite with anyone who has limited time to spend in the kitchen. This recipe is based on the Middle Eastern dish tabbouleh, and can be served as a snack, a starter, or as an accompaniment to hot dishes such as vegetable casserole, cauliflower cheese, and so on.

Preparation time: 10 minutes (plus standing time for bulgur)
Cooking time: None

METRIC/IMPERIAL	AMERICAN
115g/4 oz bulgur	½ cup bulgur
1 courgette, coarsely grated	1 zucchini, coarsely grated
½ small cauliflower, divided into florets	½ small cauliflower, divided into florets
2 spring onions, chopped	2 scallions, chopped
2 large tomatoes, chopped	2 large tomatoes, chopped
1 avocado, stoned, peeled and chopped	1 avocado, pitted, peeled and chopped
55g/2 oz walnuts, chopped	½ cup walnuts, chopped
2 tablespoons chopped fresh parsley	2 tablespoons chopped fresh parsley
2 tablespoons chopped fresh mint	2 tablespoons chopped fresh mint
2 tablespoons olive oil	2 tablespoons olive oil
2 tablespoons lemon juice	2 tablespoons lemon juice
seasoning to taste	seasoning to taste
lemon wedges to garnish	lemon wedges to garnish

1 Put the bulgur into a bowl, cover with boiling water and leave for 30 minutes (or use cold water and leave for 1 hour). Drain the bulgur, then either put it into a clean tea towel and pat dry, or put it into a colander and press it gently against the side.
2 In a bowl, combine the bulgur, courgette (zucchini), cauliflower florets, spring onions (scallions), tomatoes, avocado and walnuts. Whisk together the herbs, oil, lemon juice and seasoning and pour this dressing over the salad. Toss gently.
3 If time allows, cover and chill the salad briefly before serving. It can even be left overnight.

TIP Any leftovers can be used as a stuffing for baked vegetables such as peppers. Vary the salad in winter by mixing the bulgur with finely chopped or grated parsnip, leeks or mushrooms, maybe adding some raisins or chopped apple, and flavouring the dressing with spices instead of herbs.

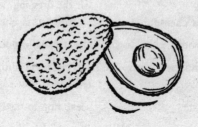

Three-bean Salad with Blue Cheese Dressing

———————

Though full of protein and very satisfying, bean salads can be a bit unexciting. Not this one though, with its tangy dressing that includes yogurt (the perfect aid to digestion!).

Preparation time: 10 minutes (plus chilling)
Cooking time: A few minutes

METRIC/IMPERIAL	AMERICAN
225g/8 oz green beans	½ pound green beans
395g/14 oz can chick peas	1 medium can garbanzo beans
395g/14 oz can kidney beans	1 medium can kidney beans
½ small cucumber, diced	½ small cucumber, diced
1 small yellow pepper, diced	1 small yellow pepper, diced

For the dressing	**For the dressing**
85g/3 oz ricotta cheese	⅓ cup ricotta cheese
about 6 tablespoons plain yogurt	about 6 tablespoons plain yogurt
1 tablespoon chopped fresh chives	1 tablespoon chopped fresh chives
seasoning to taste	seasoning to taste
55g/2 oz blue cheese, crumbled	¼ cup blue cheese, crumbled

1 Trim the green beans, cut them into chunks, and cook in a saucepan of boiling water for just a few minutes. They should be tender but still quite firm. Drain well and put into a bowl.
2 Stir in the drained chick peas (garbanzo beans) and kidney beans and the diced cucumber and yellow pepper.
3 In another bowl, mix together the dressing ingredients, using as much yogurt as needed to make a creamy but not too thick dressing. Add the blue cheese last, stirring it in gently so that it does not break up completely.
4 Stir the dressing into the beans, then cover and chill for an hour before serving. It goes well with a lettuce and watercress salad and fresh wholemeal bread.

TIP Use sieved cottage cheese or another low-fat soft cheese if you can't get ricotta. You can, of course, make the dressing smooth rather than chunky – just process it in a blender.

Spinach, Potato and Tofu Salad

V+

A lovely summer salad which uses the new season's vegetables in a way that brings out all their flavour.

Preparation time: 10 minutes (plus marinating)
Cooking time: 15 minutes

METRIC/IMPERIAL	AMERICAN
285g/10 oz tofu, drained	1¼ cups tofu, drained
140ml/¼ pt olive oil	⅔ cup olive oil
1 tablespoon cider vinegar	1 tablespoon cider vinegar
1 clove garlic, crushed	1 clove garlic, crushed
1 spring onion, finely chopped	1 scallion, finely chopped
seasoning to taste	seasoning to taste
225g/8 oz small new potatoes	½ pound small new potatoes
1 tablespoon vegetable oil	1 tablespoon vegetable oil
340g/12 oz fresh spinach leaves	¾ pound fresh spinach leaves
soya 'bacon' bits (optional)	soy 'bacon' bits (optional)

1 Cut the tofu into cubes. Lightly whisk together the olive oil, cider vinegar, garlic, spring onion (scallion) and seasoning, then pour this mixture over the tofu. Cover and leave to marinate for a few hours or overnight.

2 Scrub the potatoes and steam them for 10 minutes, or until just tender. Drain well.

3 Heat the vegetable oil in a pan and add the potatoes. Cook them gently, stirring frequently, for 5 minutes or until golden. Drain well, season and leave to cool.

4 Wash the spinach, pat dry, remove the stalks and coarsely shred the leaves. Put them in a serving bowl, stir in the potatoes and add the tofu. Drizzle a little of the marinade over the top as a dressing, and sprinkle with 'bacon' bits, if using them. Serve at once.

TIP Crunchy, salty 'bacon' bits go especially well with spinach and tofu, but if you don't like them, try using lightly roasted cashew nuts or croûtons. Or, for a peppery, spicy taste, substitute half a dozen thickly sliced radishes.

Nutmeat with Pineapple Coleslaw

Even if you're not keen on coleslaw you might like this savoury-sweet version which really is special. You can, of course, use fresh pineapple if you prefer. Add nutmeat for protein, or – if you don't have any handy – serve the coleslaw with slices of cold nut loaf, maybe left over from a previous meal. Braised tofu also goes well with this coleslaw.

Preparation time: 10 minutes
Cooking time: None

METRIC/IMPERIAL	AMERICAN
225g/8 oz can nutmeat	small can nutmeat
½ small white cabbage, finely grated	½ small white cabbage, finely grated
½ small dark green cabbage, finely grated	½ small dark green cabbage, finely grated
¼ small Spanish onion, finely grated	¼ small sweet onion, finely grated
1 large carrot, coarsely grated	1 large carrot, coarsely grated
225g/8 oz can pineapple pieces	small can pineapple pieces
mayonnaise	mayonnaise
watercress to garnish	watercress to garnish

1 Cut the nutmeat into cubes.
2 In a large bowl, mix together the two cabbages, onion and carrot. Drain the pineapple pieces and chop coarsely, then add to the vegetables, making sure everything is well mixed.
3 Stir in just enough mayonnaise to coat the vegetables very lightly (besides having a strong flavour that could easily overpower the others, too much mayonnaise can turn what should be a light and crunchy salad into a heavy sludge!).
4 Stir the nutmeat cubes into the coleslaw and garnish with watercress. Serve with warm bran muffins (page 48), for a change.

TIP Tofu mayonnaise can be used to make this recipe suitable for vegans. The coleslaw can be served to everyone in the family, the non-vegetarians adding whatever they like in place of the nutmeat. Though all salads are best eaten as soon as possible, this one will keep for a day or so if covered and stored in a cool place. Add the nutmeat just before serving.

Sweetcorn Chowder

A subtly flavoured, creamy soup based on a traditional recipe that usually includes fish. Fish eaters could, of course, add some to their portion, though it really is delicious just as it is.

Preparation time: 10 minutes
Cooking time: 20–30 minutes

METRIC/IMPERIAL	AMERICAN
2 tablespoons vegetable oil	2 tablespoons vegetable oil
1 large onion, chopped	1 large onion, chopped
340g/12 oz potatoes, cut into small cubes	¾ pound potatoes, cut into small cubes
1 large carrot, finely chopped	1 large carrot, finely chopped
1 stick celery, finely chopped	1 stick celery, finely chopped
850ml/1½ pints vegetable stock	3¾ cups vegetable stock
170g/6 oz fresh or frozen sweetcorn	1 cup fresh or frozen corn kernels
2 tablespoons wholemeal flour	2 tablespoons wholewheat flour
200ml/⅓ pint plain yogurt	¾ cup plain yogurt
seasoning to taste	seasoning to taste
2 tablespoons chopped fresh parsley	2 tablespoons chopped fresh parsley

1 Heat the oil in a large saucepan. Add the onion and cook for a few minutes, then stir in the potatoes, carrot and celery and cook for a few minutes more.
2 Stir in the stock and sweetcorn, bring to a boil, then cover the pan and lower the heat. Simmer for 10 minutes, or until the vegetables are cooked.
3 In a small bowl combine the flour and yogurt. Add this mixture to the soup and cook over a medium heat, stirring continually, until it thickens. Season well, add the parsley, and serve at once.

TIP This soup can be made suitable for vegans by simply using non-dairy yogurt, or stirring in some concentrated soya milk instead.

Carrot and Fennel Soup with Croûtons

An unusual carrot soup with a distinctive flavour – its pretty colour makes it ideal as a starter for a dinner party. You can also thicken the soup with extra flour and use it as a sauce to serve with pasta or whole grains such as rice or wheat berries.

Preparation time: 10 minutes
Cooking time: 45 minutes

METRIC/IMPERIAL	AMERICAN
2 tablespoons vegetable oil	2 tablespoons vegetable oil
1 onion, chopped	1 onion, chopped
455g/1 lb carrots, chopped	1 pound carrots, chopped
2 sticks celery, chopped	2 sticks celery, chopped
850ml/1½ pints vegetable stock	3¾ cups vegetable stock
seasoning to taste	seasoning to taste
1 teaspoon fennel seeds, or to taste	1 teaspoon fennel seeds, or to taste
200ml/⅓ pint creamy milk	¾ cup creamy milk
2 level tablespoons wholemeal flour	2 level tablespoons wholewheat flour

For the croûtons

2 slices wholemeal bread	2 slices wholewheat bread
2 tablespoons vegetable oil	2 tablespoons vegetable oil

1 Heat the oil in a saucepan, add the onion and cook for a few minutes, then add the carrots and celery and cook gently for 3 minutes more.
2 Pour in the stock, bring to a boil, then cover and simmer for 30 minutes, or until the vegetables are tender. Season well.
3 Pour the soup into a blender and process to a thick purée. Add the fennel seeds towards the end so that they are crushed but don't completely disintegrate. Transfer the mixture to a clean saucepan.
4 In a small bowl combine the milk and flour. Stir this paste into the soup and heat gently, stirring, until it thickens.
5 To make the croûtons, remove the crusts from the bread slices and cut into small, even-sized squares. Heat the oil in a frying pan, add the bread and fry, stirring continually, until crisp and nicely browned. Drain well on paper towels and either serve at once, or allow to cool and store in an airtight jar.
6 Serve the soup piping hot, and hand round the croûtons for everyone to help themselves.

TIP Coriander seeds can be substituted for fennel. Or you can omit the seeds altogether and flavour the soup with a bouquet garni or other herbs. For garlic-flavoured croûtons add a peeled, crushed clove of garlic to the frying pan with the oil, or sprinkle with garlic salt.

Chinese Cabbage Egg-drop Soup

Very quick to prepare, light and fresh-tasting, this soup – like most Chinese-style soups – is designed to stimulate the taste buds rather than fill you up. Serve it as a starter, or when the weather is too hot for anything more substantial.

Preparation time: 5 minutes
Cooking time: 15 minutes

METRIC/IMPERIAL	AMERICAN
1 litre/1¾ pints good vegetable stock	4⅓ cups good vegetable stock
2 spring onions, chopped	2 scallions, chopped
115g/4 oz button mushrooms, sliced	2 cups sliced button mushrooms
1 teaspoon lemon juice	1 teaspoon lemon juice
1 tablespoon soy sauce	1 tablespoon soy sauce
1 small Chinese cabbage, finely shredded	1 small Chinese cabbage, finely shredded
2 large free-range eggs, lightly beaten	2 large free-range eggs, lightly beaten
55g/2 oz mung bean sprouts	1 cup mung bean sprouts
seasoning to taste	seasoning to taste

1 Bring the vegetable stock to a boil in a large saucepan then add the spring onions (scallions) and mushrooms, lower the heat and simmer for 5 minutes.

2 Add the lemon juice and soy sauce, then add the shredded cabbage and cook gently for a few more minutes or until the cabbage softens.

3 Bring the soup back to a boil and slowly add the beaten eggs, stirring continually. Continue cooking just long enough for the eggs to set into fine shreds. Add the bean sprouts, season, and serve at once.

TIP Because this is such a simple soup, the quality of the vegetable stock is especially important. Nothing, of course, can beat homemade. If you get into the habit of making your own, freeze some of it in an ice-cube tray, all ready to be used when needed.

A good way to ensure the eggs break up and set in shreds is to stir them with the prongs of a fork as you pour them into the soup. Non-vegetarians might like to add shredded cooked chicken or pork to their portion.

Peanut and Onion Soup

V+

Peanuts and onions – a surprisingly delicious combination that
will appeal to everyone. For a more filling version, put a slice of
French bread in the base of each bowl and pour the soup over
the top.

Preparation time: 5 minutes
Cooking time: 35 minutes

METRIC/IMPERIAL	AMERICAN
30g/1 oz vegan margarine	2 tablespoons vegan margarine
225g/8 oz onions, finely chopped	½ pound onions, finely chopped
2 tablespoons wholemeal flour	2 tablespoons wholewheat flour
850ml/1½ pints vegetable stock	3¾ cups vegetable stock
½ teaspoon dried thyme, or to taste	½ teaspoon dried thyme, or to taste
1 bay leaf	1 bay leaf
seasoning to taste	seasoning to taste
1 teaspoon yeast extract	1 teaspoon yeast extract
3–4 tablespoons crunchy peanut butter	3–4 tablespoons crunchy peanut butter
1 tablespoon chopped fresh parsley	1 tablespoon chopped fresh parsley

1 Melt the margarine in a saucepan and gently cook the onions, stirring occasionally, for 10 minutes or until beginning to colour. Sprinkle with the flour, cook for a minute more, then add the stock, herbs, seasoning and yeast extract.
2 Bring to a boil, then cover the saucepan, lower the heat and simmer for 20 minutes. Remove the bay leaf.
3 Stir in enough peanut butter to make the soup creamy. Serve hot, garnished with the parsley.

TIP Smooth peanut butter, other nut butters or tahini can all be used instead of crunchy peanut butter. Or, unless you are cooking for vegans, omit the butters altogether, stir in a little yogurt or soured cream, and top the soup with grated cheese.

Aduki Bean Burgers

V+

Any cooked beans can be used to make burgers, but aduki are especially suitable as they have the right texture, and a rich almost 'meaty' flavour.

Preparation time: 10 minutes
Cooking time: 15 minutes

METRIC/IMPERIAL	AMERICAN
2 tablespoons vegetable oil	2 tablespoons vegetable oil
1 leek, finely chopped	1 leek, finely chopped
2 carrots, grated	2 carrots, grated
2 cloves garlic, crushed	2 cloves garlic, crushed
1 tablespoon tomato paste	1 tablespoon tomato paste
1 tablespoon chopped fresh parsley	1 tablespoon chopped fresh parsley
1 teaspoon dried marjoram	1 teaspoon dried marjoram
1 tablespoon soy sauce	1 tablespoon soy sauce
395g/14 oz can aduki beans	medium can aduki beans
115g/14 oz wholemeal breadcrumbs	3 cups wholewheat breadcrumbs
seasoning to taste	seasoning to taste
wholemeal flour	wholewheat flour
vegetable oil for frying	vegetable oil for frying
wholemeal rolls, sliced tomato and relishes to serve	wholewheat rolls, sliced tomato and relishes to serve

1 Heat the oil in a saucepan and gently fry the leek, carrots and garlic for 5 minutes or until soft. Add the tomato paste, parsley, marjoram and soy sauce, stir well and remove from the heat.
2 Drain the beans and mash to a purée. Add to the other ingredients with the breadcrumbs and seasoning. The mixture should be firm enough to shape – if it is too soft, add more breadcrumbs; if it is too dry, add a little vegetable stock or water.
3 Divide the mixture into 8, shape into burgers and coat them lightly with flour. Shallow-fry them, turning once, until brown and crisp. Tuck each one into a bread roll, top with slices of tomato and serve at once, accompanied by a choice of relishes.

TIP To save time you can leave out the initial frying: omit the leek, replace the garlic with garlic salt, use chopped nuts instead of flour as a coating, and eat the burgers raw. Excellent with salad.

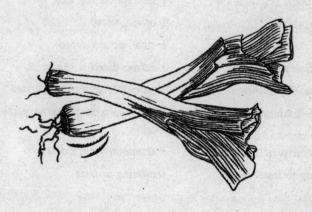

Cornish Pasties

These pasties use a TVP (Textured Vegetable Protein) filling to make them as similar as possible to the more traditional meat-filled pasties. Try them out on meat eaters and see if they can tell the difference!

Preparation time: 40 minutes (plus chilling)
Cooking time: 35–45 minutes

METRIC/IMPERIAL	AMERICAN
225g/8 oz wholemeal flour	2 cups wholewheat flour
115g/4 oz margarine	½ cup margarine
½ teaspoon mustard powder	½ teaspoon mustard powder
1 tablespoon vegetable oil	1 tablespoon vegetable oil
1 onion, sliced	1 onion, sliced
1 small potato, diced	1 small potato, diced
1 carrot, diced	1 carrot, diced
55g/2 oz TVP mince, rehydrated	½ cup TVP mince, rehydrated
about 2–3 tablespoons vegetable stock	about 2–3 tablespoons vegetable stock
1 teaspoon yeast extract	1 teaspoon yeast extract
seasoning to taste	seasoning to taste

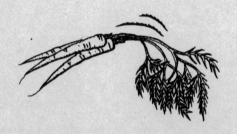

1 To make the pastry, put the flour in a bowl and rub in the margarine with your fingertips until the mixture resembles fine breadcrumbs. Stir in the mustard powder, then add about 3 tablespoons water – or just enough to make a fairly soft dough. Cover and chill for 30 minutes.

2 Meanwhile, prepare the filling. Heat the oil in a saucepan and fry the onion for a few minutes. Add the potato and carrot and cook for a further 5 minutes, stirring occasionally. Add the TVP and a few spoonfuls of vegetable stock to cover. Stir in the yeast extract, season, and cook for 5 minutes more.

3 Divide the dough into 4 pieces and on a floured board roll each one out into a circle about 15cm/6 in across. Trim the sides to make neat circles.

4 Drain any excess liquid from the filling, then spoon some into the centre of each circle. Dampen the edges with water, fold in half to make a pasty, and press the edges together to seal. Prick the tops lightly with a fork, then carefully transfer to a baking sheet.

5 Bake in the oven at 200°C/400°F (Gas Mark 6) for 20–30 minutes, or until the pastry is cooked. Serve hot, warm or cold.

TIP Use tofu or coarsely chopped nuts instead of the TVP. Or fill the pasties with vegetables in a thick curry sauce. If you are always in a rush, apart from keeping some ready-to-use pastry in the freezer there is another short cut worth taking. When you do have some minutes to spare, rub a quantity of fat into flour and store the mixture in a screwtop container in the fridge. Then when you need pastry all you need to do is add water – and you've also got an instant crumble topping for sweet or savoury dishes.

Sandwiches Unlimited

Though everyone probably takes packed lunches at some time in their lives, vegetarians may well find themselves depending on them more than most. They may still be at school or college, and find the food provided doesn't take their needs into account, or simply doesn't appeal. They may work in an office or factory and have to use a canteen where the choice is limited.

If it seems as if the vegetarian in the family is going to be restricted to cheese and tomato sandwiches, consider some of the suggestions below. They are simply ideas – combinations for you to try, and maybe adapt to create even more interesting fillings of your own.

Don't forget to be imaginative with the bread you use. Nowadays it is possible to buy all sorts of bread, and though wholemeal is nutritionally superior that doesn't mean you have to stick to it all the time. Look out for wheatgerm bread, olive bread, rye bread, Italian bread, pitta bread, Lebanese bread . . . The list goes on. Try sweet breads too, such as raisin or banana tea bread – great with creamy cheese fillings, nut butters or whole-fruit jams.

- Cottage cheese with curry paste and mango chutney
- Crumbled blue cheese with thin slices of apple or pear
- Soft white cheese with apricot jam
- Ricotta cheese with chopped dates or prunes
- Cottage cheese with honey and chopped almonds
- Garlic- and herb-flavoured hard cheese with chicory (endive) rings
- Soft white cheese with banana slices
- Gruyère cheese with red pepper rings
- Peanut butter with bean sprouts
- Tahini with chopped black olives and tomato slices
- Apple butter with chopped almonds
- Almond butter, watercress and lettuce
- Hazelnut butter, bean sprouts and cucumber.

- Scrambled eggs with chopped green pepper
- Egg mayonnaise with avocado slices
- Hard-boiled egg in curry sauce with tomatoes
- Yeast extract, grated courgette (zucchini) and chopped nuts
- Braised tofu with celery slices
- Mashed tofu fried with onion
- Smoked tofu slices with lettuce and mustard and cress
- Banana with chopped dates and desiccated (shredded) coconut
- Banana with maple syrup
- Left-over nut or bean loaf slices with grated cabbage
- Hummus with chopped olives and fennel
- Avocado with crumbled tortilla chips

TRADITIONAL MEALS
THE VEGETARIAN WAY

Evening meals, weekend meals, meals shared with guests – times when the whole family may come together – these are the occasions when special care needs to be taken if everything is to go smoothly.

Although based on meat and fish dishes, the recipes that follow are different. They require a little extra time in the kitchen, and some contain unusual ingredients. You'll also find many of these recipes can be adapted so that, although everyone may appear to be eating much the same thing, one version is for the vegetarians and one for everyone else. As not all vegetarians want to spend the whole meal justifying why they eat the way they do, these can be especially useful. (Just make sure you know which is which when you serve them!)

There are numerous variations on this mix and match theme. You could choose the dishes so that the main courses – one vegetarian, one not – can both be served with the same accompaniments. Even better, the two dishes should be able to share the oven, or if the vegetarian dish is prepared in advance it could be heated up in a microwave. Alternatively, you might like to serve the vegetarian dish as an accompaniment to whatever everyone else is having.

The first part of this chapter consists of dishes that are simple, quick and inexpensive to prepare. Following are special-occasion dishes that require a little extra effort, but are well worth it. When serving these, do remember the importance of using attractive dishes and garnishes.

Everyday Dishes

Beany Shepherd's Pie

V+

Field beans are a kind of broad bean (fava bean), and they're one of the cheapest beans you can buy. They've also got a heavy texture and rich taste, so are an ideal bean to use when you want a meaty feel to a dish. Of course, if you can't get them or don't like them, you can use other beans in the same way.

Preparation time: 10 minutes (plus soaking overnight)
Cooking time: 1 hour 15 minutes

METRIC/IMPERIAL	AMERICAN
115g/4 oz field beans, soaked overnight	½ cup field beans, soaked overnight
455g/1 lb potatoes, diced	1 pound potatoes, diced
2 tablespoons vegetable oil	2 tablespoons vegetable oil
1 large onion, chopped	1 large onion, chopped
2 sticks celery, chopped	2 sticks celery, chopped
2 tablespoons wholemeal flour	2 tablespoons wholewheat flour
200ml/⅓ pint vegetable stock	¾ cup vegetable stock
½ teaspoon dried basil	½ teaspoon dried basil
2 teaspoons dried rosemary, crushed	2 teaspoons dried rosemary, crushed
seasoning to taste	seasoning to taste
1 teaspoon yeast extract, or to taste	1 teaspoon yeast extract, or to taste
55g/2 oz vegan margarine	¼ cup vegan margarine

1 Drain the beans, cover with fresh water, then bring to a boil and continue boiling for 10 minutes. Cover the saucepan, lower the heat and cook gently for approximately 1 hour, or until tender. Drain well. When cool, mash coarsely.
2 Meanwhile, steam the potatoes until tender, then set aside. Heat the oil in a frying pan, add the onion and celery and fry gently for 5 minutes, or until the onion begins to brown. Sprinkle in the flour, cook for 1 more minute, then pour in the stock and simmer until the sauce thickens.
3 Stir the beans into the sauce with the herbs, seasoning and yeast extract. Simmer gently for 5 more minutes.
4 Meanwhile, quickly mash the potatoes with half the margarine. Transfer the filling to an ovenproof dish and cover with the potato, using a fork to pattern the top. Dot with the remaining margarine, and put under a hot grill (broiler). Serve as soon as the top colours.

TIP This dish can be made in considerably less time if you cook the beans in advance – something that's well worth doing, especially if you cook up extra for use another time. Traditionally shepherd's pie is baked in the oven. It will need 20–30 minutes at 200°C/400°F (Gas Mark 6). Try it, too, sprinkled with grated cheese or sunflower seeds. Substitute puréed parsnips for the potato topping, or combine potatoes with mashed swede (rutabaga).

Savoury Suet Pudding

V+

With a tasty and satisfying winter dish like this on the menu, who needs meat?

Preparation time: 15 minutes (plus soaking time for barley)
Cooking time: 3½ hours

METRIC/IMPERIAL	AMERICAN
1 large onion, sliced	1 large onion, sliced
2 leeks, sliced	2 leeks, sliced
2 carrots, sliced	2 carrots, sliced
115g/4 oz pot barley, soaked	½ cup pot barley, soaked
285ml/½ pint vegetable stock	1½ cups vegetable stock
1 teaspoon dried mixed herbs	1 teaspoon dried mixed herbs
395g/14 oz can black-eyed peas	medium can black-eyed peas
seasoning to taste	seasoning to taste
285g/10 oz wholemeal flour	2½ cups wholewheat flour
2 teaspoons baking powder	2 teaspoons baking powder
150g/5 oz vegetable suet, grated	⅔ cup vegetarian suet, grated

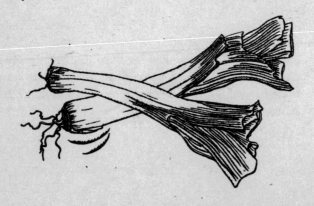

1 In a large saucepan, combine the onion, leeks, carrots, barley, vegetable stock and herbs. Bring to a boil, then cover and simmer for 15 minutes.

2 Add the black-eyed peas and cook for 15 minutes longer, or until all the vegetables are tender. Season generously.

3 Sift together the flour and baking powder, then use a fork to mix in the suet. Add enough cold water to make a firm dough. Roll out three quarters of this and use to line a 1.15l/2 pint/5 cup basin, trimming the edges.

4 Use a slotted spoon to transfer the vegetables, barley and black-eyed peas to the bowl, adding just enough liquid to keep them moist (too much will seep through the pastry). Top the pudding with the remaining pastry and press the edges together to seal.

5 Cover with lightly oiled greaseproof paper plus a layer of foil, pleating the paper across the top to allow room for the pudding to rise. Tie securely around the top with string. Stand the basin in a large saucepan and pour in boiling water to come just over half way up the sides of the basin. Cover with a lid and simmer gently for 3 hours, checking frequently to see if more hot water is needed (never let the pudding boil dry).

6 To serve, remove the layers of paper and place a plate over the top, then carefully invert the bowl and plate so that the pudding is upside down. Remove the basin and cut the pudding into slices. Serve with potatoes.

TIP Suet puddings are very slow cooking, but perfect if you want to get the meal going early in the day. You can also cook potatoes and other vegetables in the same pan by putting them into a steamer suspended above the pudding – add towards the end of the cooking time. Alternatively you could make individual puddings, adding meat to some of them. This will reduce the cooking by an hour or so.

Chilli Non Carne

V+

This chilli sauce can be used as the basis for chilli con carne (with meat) too. Though adding TVP gives the vegetarian version a more authentic texture, you can omit it if you prefer, and double the amount of kidney beans.

Preparation time: 10 minutes
Cooking time: 35 minutes

METRIC/IMPERIAL	AMERICAN
1 tablespoon vegetable oil	1 tablespoon vegetable oil
1 onion, chopped	1 onion, chopped
1–2 cloves garlic, crushed	1–2 cloves garlic, crushed
395g/14 oz can tomatoes, chopped	medium can tomatoes, chopped
2 tablespoons tomato paste	2 tablespoons tomato paste
1–2 teaspoons chilli powder, or to taste	1–2 teaspoons chilli powder, or to taste
¼ teaspoon ground cumin	¼ teaspoon ground cumin
seasoning to taste	seasoning to taste
150g/5 oz TVP mince, rehydrated in vegetable stock or water	1¼ cups TVP mince, rehydrated in vegetable stock or water
200g/7 oz can kidney beans	small can kidney beans

1 Heat the oil in a saucepan and lightly fry the onion and garlic for 5 minutes.
2 Stir in the tomatoes, tomato paste, chilli powder, cumin, seasoning and TVP mince. Bring to a boil then lower the heat, cover the pan, and simmer gently for 20 minutes.
3 Drain the kidney beans and add to the pan. Stir, then continue cooking gently for 10 minutes. Serve with rice, or as a filling for taco shells.

TIP You can use plain or flavoured TVP for this recipe. If you like chilli you can use fresh chilli peppers. These vary enormously in strength, but as a general rule the long pods are hotter than the round ones and the red are hotter than the green.

Lentil and Walnut Risotto

V+

Though traditionally made with a special short grain rice, risottos can also be made with long grain white or brown rice, plus a combination of whatever vegetables you have handy, fresh or frozen. This version is a subtly flavoured vegan risotto. You can also add garlic, onion, herbs and, for a vegetarian topping, grated Parmesan cheese or slices of hard-boiled egg. Non-vegetarians could, of course, add meat or fish to their portion.

Preparation time: 10 minutes (plus soaking time for lentils)
Cooking time: 1 hour

METRIC/IMPERIAL	AMERICAN
85g/3 oz green lentils, soaked overnight	⅓ cup green lentils, soaked overnight
2 tablespoons vegetable oil	2 tablespoons vegetable oil
1 large leek, sliced	1 large leek, sliced
1 red pepper, sliced	1 red pepper, sliced
115g/4 oz mushrooms, sliced	2 cups sliced mushrooms
225g/8 oz brown rice	1 cup brown rice
425ml/¾ pint hot vegetable stock	2 cups hot vegetable stock
85g/3 oz walnuts, coarsely chopped	⅔ cup coarsely chopped walnuts
seasoning to taste	seasoning to taste
2 tablespoons chopped fresh parsley	2 tablespoons chopped fresh parsley
2 tomatoes, sliced	2 tomatoes, sliced

1 Drain the lentils, cover with fresh water and bring to a boil, then cover and simmer for about 20 minutes, or until beginning to soften. Drain well.

2 Meanwhile, in another pan heat the oil and add the leek and red pepper. Cook for 5 minutes then stir in the mushrooms and rice and cook for 5 minutes more, stirring frequently.

3 Pour on half the stock and simmer uncovered until the liquid has been absorbed. Add a little more, plus the drained lentils. Continue cooking until the rice is tender but not soggy, adding more liquid as necessary. You shouldn't need to drain off any excess liquid, but if it is too wet, do so.

4 Stir in the walnuts, season well, and add the parsley. Pile the mixture into a serving dish, decorate with the tomato slices, and serve at once.

TIP Allowing the rice to soak up the liquid gradually like this is the traditional way of cooking risotto, and the resulting mixture is a moister dish than is usual, though the rice should still have bite. You can, of course, use quick-cooking rice instead, in which case add all the liquid at once, then drain off any excess when the rice and lentils are tender.

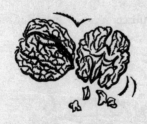

Toad in the Hole

This is a real family favourite, and especially easy to adapt if you use vegetarian sausages. If you decide to make two different versions, try making individual servings in Yorkshire pudding tins or large bun tins – making sure you know which is which!

Preparation time: 5 minutes (plus optional standing time for batter)
Cooking time: 30 minutes

METRIC/IMPERIAL	AMERICAN
115g/4 oz wholemeal flour	1 cup wholewheat flour
140ml/¼ pint milk	⅔ cup milk
140ml/¼ pint water	⅔ cup water
1 large free-range egg, lightly beaten	1 large free-range egg, lightly beaten
½ small onion, finely chopped (optional)	½ small onion, finely chopped (optional)
seasoning to taste	seasoning to taste
6 vegetarian sausages (see Tip below), canned or frozen	6 vegetarian sausages (see Tip below), canned or frozen

1 Mix together the flour, milk, water and egg, then beat to make a thick smooth batter. Add the onion and seasoning. If time allows, leave the batter to stand in a cool place for 30 minutes.
2 Lightly grease 12 Yorkshire pudding tins. Cut the sausages diagonally into 4 pieces each, then put 2 into each of the tins. Pour some of the batter over each.
3 Bake in the oven at 425°C/220°F (Gas Mark 7) for 20–30 minutes, or until the puddings are well risen. Serve at once with vegetables.

TIP How many sausages you use (and how many pieces you cut them into) will depend on their size. You can also use dry sausage or burger mixes, shaping them into sausages or balls, but don't forget to fry them first. Alternatively, fill the tins with beans, mushrooms and tomatoes instead of sausages. The batter can also be cooked in one large tin, in which case add an extra egg.

Spanish Omelette

If you think of omelettes as being too light for a main meal, try this version. Simplicity itself to make, it has a quiche-like consistency that's surprisingly filling.

Preparation time: 10 minutes
Cooking time: 15 minutes

METRIC/IMPERIAL	AMERICAN
2 tablespoons vegetable oil	2 tablespoons vegetable oil
3 spring onions, chopped	3 scallions, chopped
1 small red pepper, chopped	1 small red pepper, chopped
2 tomatoes, skinned and chopped	2 tomatoes, skinned and chopped
1 potato, cooked and diced	1 potato, cooked and diced
2 tablespoons peas, cooked	2 tablespoons peas, cooked
6 free-range eggs, separated	6 free-range eggs, separated
seasoning to taste	seasoning to taste

1 Heat the oil in a frying pan and gently fry the spring onions (scallions) and red pepper for 5 minutes, or until they begin to soften. Add the tomatoes and potato and cook a few minutes longer, then stir in the peas.
2 Meanwhile, whisk the egg whites until stiff, then lightly beat the egg yolks and seasoning and carefully fold them into the whites. Pour this mixture over the vegetables and continue cooking over a medium heat, loosening the sides with a spatula as the egg sets.
3 When the bottom of the omelette is set and the top fluffs up, place the pan under a preheated grill (broiler) and cook until the top of the omelette begins to brown. Serve cut into wedges.

TIP Meat eaters could add a sprinkling of crumbled bacon to their wedge, or serve it with a slice of cold meat.

Seitan Nuggets

Seitan is a flavoured wheat protein that originated in the Far East and has a texture not unlike chicken. You'll find it in speciality shops and wholefood stores. Seitan nuggets can be served in the same way as chicken ones – quick to prepare, they go well with potatoes and other vegetables.

Preparation time: 5 minutes
Cooking time: 10 minutes

METRIC/IMPERIAL	AMERICAN
285g/10 oz seitan, well drained	10 ounces seitan, well drained
55g/2 oz wholemeal flour	½ cup wholewheat flour
55g/2 oz fine wholemeal breadcrumbs	1 cup fine wholewheat breadcrumbs
2 tablespoons sesame seeds	2 tablespoons sesame seeds
½ teaspoon dried oregano	½ teaspoon dried oregano
½ teaspoon dried parsley	½ teaspoon dried parsley
seasoning to taste	seasoning to taste
vegetable oil for frying	vegetable oil for frying
lemon wedges to serve	lemon wedges to serve

1 Pat the seitan with paper towels so that it is as dry as possible, then cut into small, even-sized pieces. Mix the flour with just enough water to make a thick paste.
2 Combine the breadcrumbs, sesame seeds, herbs and seasoning. Dip the seitan pieces into the flour paste and then into the breadcrumb mixture, making sure they are well coated. Deep-fry or shallow-fry them in hot oil until brown and crisp.
3 Drain well on paper towels and serve accompanied with lemon wedges and vegetables.

Smoked Cheddar and Broccoli Quiche

This really tasty quiche should appeal to everyone, especially with its light pastry. A classic Quiche Lorraine can be made from the same recipe – just omit the broccoli, replace the smoked Cheddar cheese with Gruyère, and add bacon.

Preparation time: 20 minutes (plus chilling)
Cooking time: 1 hour

METRIC/IMPERIAL	AMERICAN
For the pastry	**For the pastry**
85g/3 oz wholemeal flour	¾ cup wholewheat flour
85g/3 oz plain white flour	¾ cup all-purpose flour
1 small free-range egg, beaten	1 small free-range egg, beaten
2 tablespoons vegetable oil	2 tablespoons vegetable oil
For the filling	**For the filling**
225g/8 oz broccoli florets, fresh or frozen	½ pound broccoli florets, fresh or frozen
285ml/½ pint creamy milk	1¼ cups creamy milk
2 large free-range eggs, beaten	2 large free-range eggs, beaten
115g/4 oz smoked Cheddar cheese, grated	1 cup grated smoked Cheddar cheese
seasoning to taste	seasoning to taste

1 To make the pastry, sift the flours together in a bowl. Mix the egg and oil and add to the flour with a spoonful or two of cold water – the dough should be smooth and firm. Knead briefly then wrap in foil and chill for 30 minutes.
2 Meanwhile, cook the broccoli florets in boiling water for 5 minutes or until just tender. Drain very well.
3 Beat together the milk, eggs, grated cheese and seasoning.
4 Roll out the pastry and use to line a 20cm/8 in flan dish or pie plate. Cover with silver foil or greaseproof paper, fill with dried beans, and bake in the oven at 200°C/400°F (Gas Mark 6) for 15 minutes. Carefully remove the beans and the paper. Reduce the oven temperature to 190°C/375°F (Gas Mark 5).
5 Arrange the broccoli florets in the pastry case then pour on the egg and cheese mixture. Bake for 30–40 minutes, or until set.

TIP This pastry is especially light. The base is baked 'blind', as the filling is rather liquid and may seep through if the pastry isn't cooked. The beans help prevent the pastry lifting and buckling. If using different fillings – one for vegetarians and one for non-vegetarians – you could use 4 small dishes to make individual quiches.

Eggs Florentine

Not everyone likes spinach, but those who do usually can't get enough of it! If someone in your house is a spinach fan, this simple dish is useful for quick lunches.

Preparation time: 10 minutes
Cooking time: 25–30 minutes

METRIC/IMPERIAL	AMERICAN
680g/1½ lb fresh spinach, washed and shredded	1½ pounds fresh spinach, washed and shredded
30g/1 oz margarine	2 tablespoons margarine
2 tablespoons vegetable oil	2 tablespoons vegetable oil
30g/1 oz wholemeal flour	¼ cup wholewheat flour
285g/½ pint milk	1¼ cups milk
¼ teaspoon ground nutmeg	¼ teaspoon ground nutmeg
seasoning to taste	seasoning to taste
6 free-range eggs	6 free-range eggs
2 tablespoons grated Parmesan cheese	2 tablespoons grated Parmesan cheese
2 tablespoons wholemeal breadcrumbs	2 tablespoons wholewheat breadcrumbs
3 tomatoes, quartered, to garnish	3 tomatoes, quartered, to garnish

1 Melt the margarine in a saucepan, then add the spinach with just the water that remains on the leaves after washing. Cover and cook for 5 minutes or until the spinach softens.
2 Meanwhile, heat the oil in another pan, sprinkle in the flour and cook briefly. Stir in the milk, nutmeg and seasoning and cook gently until the sauce thickens.
3 Cook the eggs in a pan of boiling water for 10 minutes. Cool slightly, then shell and halve the eggs.
4 Arrange the drained spinach in an ovenproof dish, place the eggs on top then pour on the sauce. Sprinkle with the Parmesan cheese and breadcrumbs. Put under a preheated grill (broiler) for 5–10 minutes or until the crumbs are crisp. Serve at once, garnished with the tomato quarters.

TIP Obviously this dish can easily be adapted to make tuna florentine for those who want it. If doing this, put the vegetarian version in a small dish or ramekin and grill separately.

Bean and Aubergine (Eggplant) Pies

V+

The tahini sauce gives this combination of beans and vegetables a creamy, nutty taste, a perfect contrast to the puff pastry. Shortcrust can be used instead, or for especially delicate little pies, use filo pastry.

Preparation time: 20 minutes (plus salting the aubergine (eggplant))
Cooking time: 30 minutes

METRIC/IMPERIAL	AMERICAN
1 small aubergine, diced	1 small eggplant, diced
3 tablespoons vegetable oil	3 tablespoons vegetable oil
1 large onion, sliced	1 large onion, sliced
1 clove garlic, crushed	1 clove garlic, crushed
1 red pepper, sliced	1 red pepper, sliced
30g/1 oz wholemeal flour	¼ cup wholewheat flour
285ml/½ pint vegetable stock	1½ cups vegetable stock
4 tablespoons tahini, or to taste	4 tablespoons tahini, or to taste
2 tablespoons chopped fresh chives	2 tablespoons chopped fresh chives
seasoning to taste	seasoning to taste
395g/14 oz can butter beans, drained	1 medium can butter beans, drained
225g/8 oz vegan frozen puff pastry	½ pound vegan frozen puff pastry
soya milk to glaze	soya milk to glaze
2 tablespoons sesame seeds	2 tablespoons sesame seeds

1 Sprinkle the diced aubergine (eggplant) with salt and leave in a colander for 30 minutes to remove the bitter juices, then rinse with cold water and drain. Dry the aubergine (eggplant) well after rinsing.

2 Heat 2 tablespoons of the oil in a frying pan, add the onion, garlic, red pepper and aubergine (eggplant), and cook for 10 minutes, stirring frequently, until the vegetables soften.

3 Meanwhile, make the tahini sauce. Heat the remaining oil in a clean saucepan, add the flour and cook for a few minutes. Then stir in the stock and bring to a boil. When the sauce thickens, add tahini to taste, plus the chives and seasoning.

4 Add the cooked vegetables to the sauce, stir well, then add the butter beans. Spoon into 4 individual pie dishes.

5 Roll out the pastry. Dampen the rims of the dishes, cut narrow strips of pastry, and press these against the rims. Cut 4 circles out of the remaining pastry and lay these over the top of the pies, pressing the edges to seal. Prick the pastry with a fork, then brush with milk and sprinkle with the sesame seeds.

6 Bake in the oven at 220°C/425°F (Gas Mark 7) for about 20 minutes, or until the pastry is well risen and beginning to colour. Serve at once.

TIP You can, of course, use dairy milk for glazing if you are not catering for vegans. When making individual pies like this, you might like to freeze some of them for use another day. If so, cool the filling before covering with the pastry, then freeze once you have added the pastry. You can also make a large pie using the same filling and pastry – it may need a little longer in the oven.

Mediterranean Pasta Bake with Tofu

V+

Whoever said tofu was boring? Not when cooked in a dish that's full of Mediterranean flavours. If you like, use smoked tofu rather than plain, for a flavour reminiscent of smoked fish.

Preparation time: 10 minutes
Cooking time: 35 minutes

METRIC/IMPERIAL	AMERICAN
225g/8 oz pasta shells, preferably wholemeal	4 cups pasta shells, preferably wholewheat
285g/10 oz tofu, drained	1¼ cups tofu, drained
3 tablespoons olive oil	3 tablespoons olive oil
1 large onion, sliced	1 large onion, sliced
1–2 cloves garlic, crushed	1–2 cloves garlic, crushed
1 courgette, diced	1 zucchini, diced
¼ fennel bulb, chopped	¼ fennel bulb, chopped
395g/14 oz can tomatoes, chopped	medium can tomatoes, chopped
2 teaspoons dried basil	2 teaspoons dried basil
seasoning to taste	seasoning to taste
4 tablespoons white wine or vegetable stock	4 tablespoons white wine or vegetable stock
12 black olives, quartered	12 black olives, quartered

1 Cook the pasta shells in a large saucepan of boiling water for 8–10 minutes or until just tender. Drain well.
2 Meanwhile, dice the tofu. Heat 1 tablespoon of the oil in a frying pan and fry the tofu, stirring frequently, until lightly browned on all sides. Remove from the pan with a slotted spoon.
3 Add the rest of the oil to the pan and fry the onion and garlic for 5 minutes to soften. Add the courgette (zucchini) and fennel, cook for 2 minutes, then stir in the tomatoes, basil, seasoning and wine or stock, together with the tofu. Cook for 5 minutes, adding more wine or stock if necessary – the sauce should be fairly liquid. Stir in the olives.
4 Put the pasta in an ovenproof dish then top with the sauce, making sure all the pasta is covered. Bake in the oven at 200°C/400°F (Gas Mark 6) for 15 minutes. Serve with a mixed salad.

TIP A generous sprinkling of grated cheese can be added (unless it is for vegans) just before the dish goes into the oven. Instead of pasta, spread the tofu and tomato mixture over some pre-cooked grains – rice is an obvious choice, but try it too with bulgur, wheat berries or millet. It also makes a tasty topping for homemade pizza.

'Beef' Hotpot

V+

Preparation time: 15 minutes
Cooking time: 1 hour

METRIC/IMPERIAL	AMERICAN
2 tablespoons vegetable oil	2 tablespoons vegetable oil
1 onion, sliced	1 onion, sliced
1 turnip, sliced	1 turnip, sliced
1 carrot, sliced	1 carrot, sliced
2 sticks celery, chopped	2 sticks celery, chopped
1 tablespoon wholemeal flour	1 tablespoon wholewheat flour
425ml/¾ pint vegetable stock	2 cups vegetable stock
1 teaspoon yeast extract	1 teaspoon yeast extract
seasoning to taste	seasoning to taste
150g/5 oz 'beef'-flavoured TVP chunks, rehydrated	1¼ cups 'beef'-flavoured TVP chunks, rehydrated
fresh parsley to garnish	fresh parsley to garnish

For the dumplings

115g/4 oz wholemeal flour	1 cup wholewheat flour
1 teaspoon baking powder	1 teaspoon baking powder
½–1 teaspoon dried mixed herbs	½–1 teaspoon dried mixed herbs
55g/2 oz vegetarian suet, grated	¼ cup vegetarian suet, grated

1 Heat the oil in a large saucepan, add the onion and cook for 5 minutes. Stir in the remaining vegetables and cook for a few minutes more. Sprinkle with the flour, cook briefly, then add the stock, yeast extract and seasoning.

2 Drain the TVP chunks and mix them into the other ingredients, then cover and cook gently for 10 minutes.

3 To make the dumplings, mix together the flour, baking powder and dried herbs. Add the suet, using a knife to blend it in, then add just enough cold water to make a soft dough. With floured hands, divide this into 8 pieces and shape into balls.

4 Raise the heat under the saucepan to bring the liquid to a fast boil (if necessary, add a little more stock first). Drop in the dumplings, and simmer for 20–30 minutes, or until everything is cooked. Serve piping hot, garnished with lots of fresh parsley.

TIP This hotpot uses winter vegetables, but you can easily adapt it by using others such as courgettes (zucchini), fennel, leeks, green beans – whatever you fancy. Add paprika, mushrooms, tomatoes and soured cream for a Hungarian style hotpot.

Special-Occasion Dishes

Cauliflower Cheese Roulade
—•◆•—

Roulades can be filled with all sorts of ingredients. This one uses the classic combination of cauliflower and cheese. Serve it with new potatoes and perhaps a tomato and fennel salad.

Preparation time: 30 minutes
Cooking time: 40 minutes

METRIC/IMPERIAL	AMERICAN
30g/1 oz margarine	2 tablespoons margarine
55g/2 oz wholemeal flour	½ cup wholewheat flour
285ml/½ pint milk	1¼ cups milk
seasoning to taste	seasoning to taste
3 large free-range eggs, separated	3 large free-range eggs, separated
1 small cauliflower, broken into small florets	1 small cauliflower, broken into small florets
1 tablespoon vegetable oil	1 tablespoon vegetable oil
1 onion, sliced	1 onion, sliced
3 tablespoons sweetcorn kernels, cooked	3 tablespoons corn kernels, cooked
85g/3 oz low-fat curd cheese or ricotta cheese	⅓ cup low-fat curd cheese or ricotta cheese
½ teaspoon dried marjoram	½ teaspoon dried marjoram
30g/1 oz Parmesan cheese, grated	¼ cup grated Parmesan cheese
watercress to garnish	watercress to garnish

1 Make the roulade first. Melt the margarine in a saucepan, stir in the flour and cook briefly, then add the milk and stir well. Cook gently until the sauce thickens, then season to taste. Remove from the heat and stir in the egg yolks.

2 Whisk the egg whites until stiff then use a metal spoon to fold the sauce into them.

3 Line a greased Swiss roll tin (jelly roll pan) with greased foil or greaseproof paper. Pour in the mixture and bake in the oven at 180°C/350°F (Gas Mark 4) for 30 minutes, or until it springs back when pressed lightly with a finger.

4 While the roulade is cooking, gently steam the cauliflower florets for a few minutes until they begin to soften. In another pan, heat the oil and fry the onion until it browns. Add the cauliflower and sweetcorn, stir and heat gently. Add the curd or ricotta cheese, marjoram and seasoning and keep the mixture warm over a low heat.

5 Carefully turn the roulade out of the tin (using the paper to help keep it from breaking) on to a clean tea towel sprinkled with the Parmesan cheese. Spread the filling over the roulade, then pick up one end of the tea towel, and gently roll up the roulade to make a thick roll. Garnish with watercress, and serve at once, cut into thick slices.

TIP Though roulades are best served at once, they can be kept warm for up to half an hour in a low oven – while everyone is eating their first course, maybe. Try using other fillings, such as flageolet beans in thick tomato sauce, or celery and almonds in a white sauce. Also delicious with 55g/2 oz spinach, cooked and chopped, added to the roulade itself.

Tofu Moussaka
———◆•◆———

All the delicious, rich flavours you'd expect to find in this popular Greek dish, but without the meat. As tofu is so easy to use, this version takes a surprisingly short time to put together.

Preparation time: 10 minutes (plus salting the aubergines (eggplants))
Cooking time: 1 hour

METRIC/IMPERIAL	AMERICAN
2 aubergines, thinly sliced	2 eggplants, thinly sliced
3 tablespoons olive oil	3 tablespoons olive oil
1 onion, chopped	1 onion, chopped
8 tomatoes, coarsely chopped	8 tomatoes, coarsely chopped
1 teaspoon dried thyme	1 teaspoon dried thyme
285g/10 oz tofu, drained	1¼ cups tofu, drained
55g/2 oz pumpkin seeds	½ cup pumpkin seeds
seasoning to taste	seasoning to taste
1 large free-range egg, beaten	1 large free-range egg, beaten
285ml/½ pint milk	1¼ cups milk
2 tablespoons dried wholemeal breadcrumbs	2 tablespoons dried wholewheat breadcrumbs

1 Lay the aubergine (eggplant) slices out on a colander, sprinkle with salt and leave for 30 minutes. Then rinse in cold water, drain well, and pat dry.
2 Heat half the oil in a saucepan and fry the onion for 5 minutes, then stir in the tomatoes and thyme and continue simmering for a further 5 minutes. Mash the tofu coarsely and stir it into the tomato mixture with the pumpkin seeds. Season to taste.
3 In another pan, heat the remaining oil and fry the aubergine (eggplant) slices on both sides. When cooked, drain well.
4 Lightly grease a medium-sized ovenproof dish. Arrange a third of the aubergine (eggplant) slices across the base, then top with half the tomato and tofu sauce. Repeat these layers once then top with a final layer of aubergine (eggplant).
5 Whisk together the egg, milk and seasoning, and pour over the other ingredients. Sprinkle with the breadcrumbs. Bake in the oven at 180°C/350°F (Gas Mark 4) for 40 minutes, or until set. Serve with potatoes and a crisp green salad.

TIP A tasty vegan version can be made by replacing the egg and milk with a white sauce made with soya milk, flavoured with nutmeg. You can also make a vegetarian moussaka by using other ingredients instead of the tofu – for example, lentils or minced TVP.

Mixed Mushroom Stroganoff

Who'd have thought mushrooms could be so delicious? The secret is to use not just one kind but a mixture – if possible include at least three different varieties. The most widely available are button and flat mushrooms (the same variety picked at different stages). Look out, too, for chestnut mushrooms, strongly flavoured shitakes, and delicate, curly-capped oyster mushrooms.

Preparation time: 10 minutes
Cooking time: 20 minutes

METRIC/IMPERIAL	AMERICAN
15g/½ oz margarine	1 tablespoon margarine
1 tablespoon oil	1 tablespoon oil
1 large onion, sliced	1 large onion, sliced
1 large red pepper, sliced	1 large red pepper, sliced
1 clove garlic, crushed	1 clove garlic, crushed
455g/1 lb mixed mushrooms	8 cups mixed mushrooms
2 tablespoons wholemeal flour	2 tablespoons wholewheat flour
285ml/½ pint vegetable stock	1¼ cups vegetable stock
1 tablespoon tomato paste	1 tablespoon tomato paste
200ml/⅓ pint soured cream	¾ cup soured cream
55g/2 oz peas, cooked	⅓ cup peas, cooked
seasoning to taste	seasoning to taste
2 tablespoons chopped fresh parsley	2 tablespoons chopped fresh parsley

1 Heat half the margarine with the oil in a saucepan, add the onion, red pepper and garlic, and cook gently for 5 minutes to soften.
2 Stir in the mushrooms (these should be quartered if especially large). Cook, stirring occasionally, for 5 minutes, or until just tender. Do not overcook. Use a slotted spoon to remove the vegetables and keep them warm.
3 Add the remaining margarine to the pan and stir in the flour. Cook briefly, then add the stock and tomato paste and cook until the sauce thickens. Return the vegetables to the pan and heat through.
4 Off the heat, carefully stir in the soured cream and peas, season, then continue cooking over a low heat for a few more minutes. Sprinkle with the parsley and serve. Good with noodles or rice.

TIP The peas are added simply to give colour to a rather pale dish. If you don't have any handy, add a small green pepper with the red, or sprinkle with chopped spring onions (scallions).

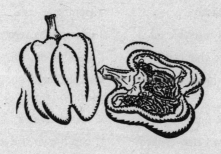

Lettuce Parcels with Creamy Carrot Sauce

V+

Rather like stuffed vine leaves (which you can use if you prefer), these rice-filled parcels are a little fiddly to prepare, but very attractive to serve. They make a delicious lunch. If you are not cooking for vegans, you can thicken the sauce with fromage frais or yogurt instead of tofu. Or serve the parcels with a spicy tomato sauce for a change.

Preparation time: 30 minutes
Cooking time: 20 minutes (or 40 minutes if using oven)

METRIC/IMPERIAL	AMERICAN
3 large carrots	3 large carrots
285ml/½ pint vegetable stock	1¼ cups vegetable stock
115g/4 oz silken tofu	½ cup silken tofu
½ teaspoon chopped fresh marjoram or tarragon	½ teaspoon chopped fresh marjoram or tarragon
seasoning to taste	seasoning to taste
2 tablespoons vegetable oil	2 tablespoons vegetable oil
1 small onion, chopped	1 small onion, chopped
85g/3 oz mushrooms, finely chopped	1½ cups finely chopped mushrooms
55g/2 oz pine nuts	½ cup pine nuts
85g/3 oz brown rice, cooked	⅓ cup brown rice, cooked
2 tablespoons chopped watercress	2 tablespoons chopped watercress
8 large lettuce leaves	8 large lettuce leaves

1 To make the sauce, slice 2 of the carrots and cook them in the stock until just tender. Cool slightly then mix with the tofu in a blender to make a creamy sauce. If necessary, add more liquid. Add the marjoram or tarragon and seasoning, and keep the sauce warm.

2 To make the stuffing, heat the oil in a clean pan and gently fry the onion for a few minutes, then stir in the mushrooms and cook for 5 minutes more.

3 Grate the remaining carrot and add to the pan with the pine nuts and well-drained rice. Heat gently, then stir in the watercress and season generously.

4 Drop the lettuce leaves into a large pan of boiling water, leave for just 30 seconds, then remove at once and rinse under cold water. Drain well and pat dry.

5 Divide the rice mixture between the lettuce leaves and fold each one into a roll, tucking in the ends to keep the filling in place. You can either serve them at once with the hot sauce, or cover the parcels and heat through in the oven at 180°C/350°F (Gas Mark 4) for 20 minutes. Serve with a crisp salad – tomatoes, fennel and olives would go well.

TIP If you don't have any cooked rice handy, try other grains such as bulgur or millet. Other nuts can replace the more expensive pine nuts – large nuts should be chopped first.

Layered Pancake Pie

Most people enjoy pancakes. Here's a way of making them into the centrepiece of your meal. Once you have tried this recipe, experiment with layering the pancakes over different fillings, making sure to vary the textures as well as the flavours. For example, use a spicy lentil purée on one, crisp celery on another, nut butter on the third. You can also make sweet pancake pies in the same way.

Preparation time: 30 minutes (plus standing time for batter)
Cooking time: 20 minutes

METRIC/IMPERIAL
For the pancakes

115g/4 oz wholemeal flour

1 large free-range egg, lightly beaten

285ml/½ pint milk or milk and water mixed

vegetable oil for frying

For filling 1

1 tablespoon vegetable oil

1 small onion, sliced

455g/1 lb spinach, washed and shredded

2 tablespoons chopped walnuts

AMERICAN
For the pancakes

1 cup wholewheat flour

1 large free-range egg, lightly beaten

1¼ cups milk or milk and water mixed

vegetable oil for frying

For filling 1

1 tablespoon vegetable oil

1 small onion, sliced

1 pound spinach, washed and shredded

2 tablespoons chopped walnuts

For filling 2

15g/½ oz margarine

2 large free-range eggs, beaten

1 tablespoon chopped chives

seasoning to taste

For filling 3

1 large, ripe avocado

squeeze of lemon juice

½ small cucumber, chopped

2 spring onions, chopped

For the topping

140ml/¼ pint crème fraîche

chopped fresh parsley

For filling 2

1 tablespoon margarine

2 large free-range eggs, beaten

1 tablespoon chopped chives

seasoning to taste

For filling 3

1 large, ripe avocado

squeeze of lemon juice

½ small cucumber, chopped

2 scallions, chopped

For the topping

⅔ cup crème fraîche

chopped fresh parsley

1 To make the batter, sift the flour into a bowl, make a well in the centre and pour in the lightly beaten egg. Beat well with a wooden spoon, then slowly add the milk or milk and water, continuing to beat the batter until it is smooth. Cover and leave in the fridge for 30 minutes.

2 Heat a little oil in a medium-sized heavy-based frying pan and add a few spoonfuls of batter, tilting the pan so the mixture covers the base. Cook gently for a few minutes. When cooked underneath, toss the pancake or turn it with a spatula, and cook the other side. Use the rest of the batter in the same way until you have 4 large pancakes. Keep the pancakes warm by putting them on a plate over a pan of boiling water and covering with foil.

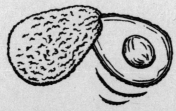

3 Prepare the fillings quickly. Heat the oil in a pan, cook the onion for a few minutes, then stir in the spinach. Cover and cook gently until it wilts. Drain well and add the walnuts.

4 In another pan, melt the margarine over a low heat, add the eggs, chives and seasoning, and cook gently, stirring continually, until just set.

5 Peel, stone and slice the avocado and sprinkle it with the lemon juice.

6 Lay one pancake on a serving dish and spread with the scrambled eggs. Top with another pancake and spread the avocado, cucumber and spring onions (scallions) over. Top with another pancake and spread with the spinach mixture, then cover with the final pancake. Dollop crème fraîche on top, sprinkle with parsley, and serve at once, cut into wedges. Good with a rice salad or new potatoes.

TIP It helps to have two cooks for this dish – one to make the pancakes while the other one prepares the fillings. Alternatively you could cook the pancakes in the morning (or even days before and freeze them) – then reheat them in the oven while preparing the fillings.

Rice and Cheese Loaf

———•◦•———

Preparation time: 10 minutes
Cooking time: 1 hour

METRIC/IMPERIAL	AMERICAN
115g/4 oz brown rice	½ cup brown rice
1 large onion, finely chopped	1 large onion, finely chopped
1 large carrot, grated	1 large carrot, grated
4 tablespoons cooked peas	4 tablespoons cooked peas
2 large free-range eggs, beaten	2 large free-range eggs, beaten
115g/4 oz mixed nuts, coarsely chopped	¾ cup coarsely chopped mixed nuts
150g/5 oz Edam cheese with herbs, grated	1¼ cups grated Edam cheese with herbs
seasoning to taste	seasoning to taste

1 Cook the rice in a saucepan of boiling water until tender then drain well.
2 In a bowl, stir together the rice, onion, carrot and peas. When well mixed, add the eggs, nuts and most of the cheese. Season generously.
3 Lightly grease a small loaf tin (pan) and spoon in the mixture, pressing it down firmly. Sprinkle with the remaining cheese.
4 Bake in the oven at 180°C/350°F (Gas Mark 4) for 30 minutes, or until set. Serve hot – it's delicious with a spicy tomato sauce. Also good cold with salad.

TIP This loaf is nutritionally balanced and therefore needs only vegetables or salad to accompany it. However, non-vegetarians might like to serve it as a side dish with meat or fish. If you only need a small portion, you could make up half the amount and shape the mixture into croquettes, then either bake or fry them.

Savoury Cheesecake

You can use ricotta cheese or Quark for this deceptively rich and
creamy cheesecake, which makes an unusual lunch dish. Other
vegetables can be used instead of the leeks. Or replace them with
cucumber and serve the cheesecake cold for a summer lunch in
the garden.

Preparation time: 15 minutes
Cooking time: 50 minutes

METRIC/IMPERIAL	AMERICAN
170g/6 oz cereal, such as Weetabix	6 ounces wholewheat cereal, such as Weetabix
85g/3 oz margarine, melted	⅓ cup margarine, melted
2 leeks, sliced	2 leeks, sliced
225g/8 oz soft cheese	2 cups soft cheese
55g/2 oz Parmesan cheese, grated	½ cup grated Parmesan cheese
6 tablespoons soured or double cream	6 tablespoons soured or heavy cream
1 tablespoon wholemeal flour	1 tablespoon wholewheat flour
1 teaspoon chopped fresh sage	1 teaspoon chopped fresh sage
seasoning to taste	seasoning to taste
3 free-range eggs, separated	3 free-range eggs, separated
55g/2 oz walnut pieces	½ cup walnut pieces

1 Crumble the cereal into a bowl, add the melted margarine and mix together well. Press the mixture evenly over the sides and base of a flan dish (tart pan) or a flan ring standing on a baking tray. Set aside.

2 Steam the leeks until just soft, then press to extract any moisture.

3 Beat together the soft cheese, Parmesan, cream, flour, sage and seasoning. Add the egg yolks. Whisk the egg whites until stiff, then use a metal spoon to fold them gently into the cheese mixture.

4 Arrange the leeks and walnut pieces on the prepared base and pour the cheese mixture over the top. Bake in the oven at 180°C/350°F (Gas Mark 4) for 45 minutes, or until set. Serve warm, cut in generous wedges, accompanied by new potatoes and a red pepper salad.

TIP To stop your cheesecake cracking across the top, leave it to cool slightly in the oven, door ajar, before serving. If you intend to eat it cold, refrigerate it for a few hours first. You can even make it a day ahead if that suits you better.

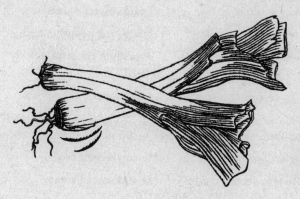

Courgette (Zucchini) Lasagne

Baked lasagne is popular with everyone, and can be made with a wide variety of fillings. This one is a summer lasagne – light, delicately flavoured, with nuts to add crunch, and a surprisingly low calorie count too.

Preparation time: 15 minutes
Cooking time: 55–65 minutes

METRIC/IMPERIAL	AMERICAN
395g/14 oz can tomatoes, chopped	medium can tomatoes, chopped
1 tablespoon chopped fresh parsley	1 tablespoon chopped fresh parsley
seasoning to taste	seasoning to taste
3 tablespoons vegetable oil	3 tablespoons vegetable oil
170g/6 oz lasagne sheets	6 ounces lasagne sheets
1 large onion, sliced	1 large onion, sliced
1 large red pepper, sliced	1 large red pepper, sliced
2 medium courgettes, thickly sliced	2 medium zucchini, thickly sliced
225g/8 oz cottage cheese with chives	1 cup cottage cheese with chives
85g/3 oz Parmesan cheese, grated	¾ cup grated Parmesan cheese
55g/2 oz walnut pieces	½ cup walnut pieces
140ml/¼ pint soured cream	⅔ cup soured cream

1 Put the tomatoes in a saucepan with the parsley and seasoning and cook over a medium heat to reduce the liquid.

2 Meanwhile, heat a large pan of boiling water, add 1 tablespoon of the oil, and drop in a few of the lasagne sheets. Cook for 8–10 minutes until just tender. Remove the sheets at once, rinse them with cold water, then lay them out (so that they are not touching) on a clean tea towel. Cook the remaining pasta in the same way.

3 Heat the remaining oil in a separate pan and lightly fry the onion and red pepper for 5 minutes. Add the courgette (zucchini) slices, cover the pan and cook gently for 10 minutes, or until just tender. Check that they do not burn.

4 Lightly grease a medium-sized ovenproof dish. Cover the base with a third of the lasagne, add half the tomato sauce, half the vegetables, half the cottage cheese, a good spoonful of the Parmesan and half the walnuts. Repeat these layers once, then top with a final layer of lasagne. Carefully pour the soured cream over the top, making sure it is spread evenly, and sprinkle with the remaining Parmesan.

5 Bake in the oven at 200°C/400°F (Gas Mark 6) for 20–30 minutes.

TIP Use whatever kind of lasagne you prefer for this recipe. Wholemeal contains more fibre, resulting in a heavier, more filling dish. White lasagne makes a softer-textured dish, and green lasagne is especially attractive. Look out, too, for pre-cooked lasagne, which means you can eliminate step 2; follow the instructions on the packet, and be sure to add extra liquid to the tomato sauce. This dish can be prepared a few hours or even the day before it is needed. Keep covered in the fridge until ready to bake.

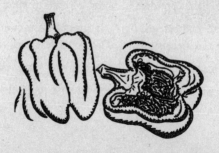

Three-Nut Loaf en Croûte with Cranberry Sauce

The classic 'alternative' Christmas dish – nut loaf served in a pastry casing and topped with cranberry sauce. If others want cranberry sauce to go with the turkey, you'll need to make extra.

Preparation time: 15 minutes
Cooking time: 40 minutes

METRIC/IMPERIAL	AMERICAN
225g/8 oz puff pastry	8 ounces puff pastry
2 tablespoons vegetable oil	2 tablespoons vegetable oil
1 onion, chopped	1 onion, chopped
1 stick celery, finely chopped	1 stick celery, finely chopped
115g/4 oz Brazil nuts, coarsely ground	¾ cup coarsely ground Brazil nuts
55g/2 oz cashew nuts, coarsely ground	½ cup coarsely ground cashew nuts
55g/2 oz hazelnuts, coarsely ground	½ cup coarsely ground hazelnuts
85g/3 oz breadcrumbs	1½ cups breadcrumbs
1 large free-range egg, beaten	1 large free-range egg, beaten
½ teaspoon ground nutmeg	½ teaspoon ground nutmeg
½ teaspoon ground cinnamon	½ teaspoon ground cinnamon
seasoning to taste	seasoning to taste
egg or milk to glaze (optional)	egg or milk to glaze (optional)
225g/8 oz fresh cranberries, or frozen cranberries, defrosted	½ pound fresh cranberries, or frozen cranberries, defrosted
55g/2 oz raw cane sugar	⅓ cup raw cane sugar
watercress to garnish	watercress to garnish

1 Roll the pastry out on a floured board to make a rectangle.

2 Heat the oil in a pan and lightly cook the onion and celery until soft. Stir in the nuts, breadcrumbs, egg, spices and seasoning. Then use your hands to shape the mixture into a loaf.

3 Place the loaf on the pastry and fold the ends over so that it is completely enclosed. Transfer to a lightly greased baking tray, making sure the join is underneath. Prick with a fork, and cut any extra pastry into shapes to decorate the top. Brush with egg or milk to glaze, if liked. Bake in the oven at 200°C/400°F (Gas Mark 6) for 30 minutes, or until puffed up and golden.

4 Meanwhile, put the cranberries, sugar and a few spoonfuls of water into a saucepan, bring to a boil, then simmer for 10 minutes. Sieve to remove the skins, then reheat gently. Add a little more water, if necessary, so that the sauce is pouring consistency.

5 Serve the nut loaf garnished with watercress, and cut into slices at the table. Pour the sauce into a warmed jug and hand it round separately.

TIP This makes 4 good servings. If only one or two people are eating it, keep the rest to eat cold another day. Alternatively, make individual portions, wrapping each one in pastry. You can add cheese to the basic nut mix, if you like. For vegans, omit the egg and add a little vegetable stock to keep the mixture moist.

Tagliatelle with Spinach and Ricotta Balls

———————

Either serve these balls to the vegetarian in place of real meat balls
(which would also go well with tagliatelle and tomato sauce), or
serve them – with a smaller portion of pasta – to everyone as a
starter.

Preparation time: 15 minutes
Cooking time: 30 minutes

METRIC/IMPERIAL	AMERICAN
30g/1 oz margarine	2 tablespoons margarine
1 clove garlic, crushed	1 clove garlic, crushed
680g/1½ lb fresh spinach, well washed and shredded	1½ pounds fresh spinach, well washed and shredded
1 large free-range egg, beaten	1 large free-range egg, beaten
55g/2 oz dried wholemeal breadcrumbs	½ cup dried wholewheat breadcrumbs
225g/8 oz ricotta cheese	1 cup ricotta cheese
55g/2 oz Parmesan cheese, grated, plus extra for serving	½ cup grated Parmesan cheese, plus extra for serving
½ teaspoon ground cumin	½ teaspoon ground cumin
seasoning to taste	seasoning to taste
1 tablespoon vegetable oil	1 tablespoon vegetable oil
455g/1 lb tagliatelle	8 cups tagliatelle
395g/14 oz can tomatoes, chopped	medium can tomatoes, chopped
1 tablespoon chopped fresh parsley	1 tablespoon chopped fresh parsley
seasoning to taste	seasoning to taste

1 Melt the margarine in a pan, add the garlic and shredded spinach, and stir over a medium heat for 5 minutes or until the spinach wilts. Drain it well, squeezing to remove as much moisture as possible. Chop finely.

2 Mix together the spinach, egg, breadcrumbs, ricotta and Parmesan cheeses, cumin and seasoning, stirring until the mixture is smooth.

3 With floured hands, take small pieces of the mixture and roll them into balls. Drop them, a few at a time, into a large saucepan of boiling water, lower the heat to a simmer and cook gently for 5–10 minutes, or until they rise to the surface. Remove the cooked balls with a slotted spoon and keep them warm while using the rest of the mixture in the same way.

4 Meanwhile, bring another pan of water to the boil, add the vegetable oil then the tagliatelle, and cook for about 10 minutes, or until just tender. Drain well.

5 To make tomato sauce, put the tomatoes in a saucepan with the parsley and seasoning and cook over a medium heat to reduce the liquid.

6 Divide the pasta between 4 plates, spoon on some of the tomato sauce, and serve topped with the spinach and ricotta balls. Hand round extra Parmesan cheese. Serve at once.

TIP To make the spinach and ricotta mixture easier to handle, chill it for 30 minutes or longer before cooking. You can make it in the morning, saving you valuable time in the evening – especially if you also have some tomato sauce in the freezer!

Marrow Cobbler

A nice old-fashioned dish for an autumn evening when it's cold outside and everyone is starving! The cobbler topping can also be used with a vegetable mix – add yogurt to the sauce for extra protein, or maybe some cooked beans.

Preparation time: 15 minutes
Cooking time: 35 minutes

METRIC/IMPERIAL	AMERICAN
For the topping	**For the topping**
170g/6 oz wholemeal flour	1½ cups wholewheat flour
2 teaspoons baking powder	2 teaspoons baking powder
1 teaspoon mustard powder	1 teaspoon mustard powder
2 teaspoons dried mixed herbs	2 teaspoons dried mixed herbs
55g/2 oz margarine	¼ cup margarine
6 tablespoons milk	6 tablespoons milk
55g/2 oz Red Leicester or Cheddar cheese, grated	½ cup grated Red Leicester or Cheddar cheese
For the filling	**For the filling**
140g/5 oz 'beef'-flavoured TVP chunks, rehydrated	1¼ cups 'beef'-flavoured TVP chunks, rehydrated
2 tablespoons vegetable oil	2 tablespoons vegetable oil
1 large onion, sliced	1 large onion, sliced
1 small marrow, diced	1 small marrow, diced
1 tablespoon wholemeal flour	1 tablespoon wholewheat flour
140ml/¼ pint vegetable stock	⅔ cup vegetable stock
½ teaspoon dried marjoram	½ teaspoon dried marjoram
soy sauce to taste	soy sauce to taste

seasoning to taste	seasoning to taste
4 tomatoes, chopped	4 tomatoes, chopped

1 Sift together the flour, baking powder, mustard powder and herbs. Use your fingertips to rub in the margarine until the mixture is like fine breadcrumbs. Add just enough milk to bind to a soft but not too sticky dough. Wrap in foil and chill for 30 minutes.

2 Drain the TVP. Heat the oil in a pan and fry the onion for 5 minutes to soften. Stir in the TVP and the marrow, and cook for 5 more minutes, stirring frequently. Sprinkle with the flour, cook briefly, then add the stock and marjoram and bring to a boil. Add soy sauce to taste, then season and simmer for another 5 minutes. Stir in the tomatoes and transfer the mixture to an ovenproof dish.

3 On a lightly floured surface, roll out the dough – it doesn't need to be very thin. Cut out small circles, or cut into fingers. Arrange these on top of the filling and sprinkle with the cheese. Bake in the oven at 220°C/425°F (Gas Mark 7) for 10–15 minutes, or until the topping is cooked. Serve at once with green vegetables.

TIP Cook the cobbler in individual dishes if you prefer, then you can use a variety of fillings. Cut out the topping with a fluted cutter to make it look extra special.

Vegetarian Kebabs

Kebabs can be made with a variety of vegetarian ingredients. Delicious hot or cold, as a main meal or as part of a buffet, they're also ideal to serve at a barbecue. Each of the versions below makes 4 kebabs – serve 2 per person for a main course.

Preparation time: 5–15 minutes
Cooking time: 5–15 minutes

METRIC/IMPERIAL

Version 1

225g/8 oz Mozzarella cheese, diced

1 large avocado, peeled, stoned and diced

1 red pepper, diced

vegetable oil

garlic salt

paprika

Version 2

225g/8 oz smoked tofu, drained and diced

1 large green pepper, diced

8 cherry tomatoes

4 baby sweetcorn, cut into chunks

1 small aubergine, diced

1 small sweet onion, thickly sliced

AMERICAN

Version 1

8 ounces Mozzarella cheese, diced

1 large avocado, peeled, pitted and diced

1 red pepper, diced

vegetable oil

garlic salt

paprika

Version 2

1 cup smoked tofu, drained and diced

1 large green pepper, diced

8 cherry tomatoes

4 baby sweetcorn, cut into chunks

1 small eggplant, diced

1 small sweet onion, thickly sliced

bay leaves	bay leaves
vegetable oil	vegetable oil
seasoning to taste	seasoning to taste

1 Simply thread the prepared ingredients on to skewers, arranging them to make an interesting colour combination. Brush everything lightly with oil, adding seasoning as liked.
2 Cook them under a medium grill (or over a barbecue) for 5–15 minutes, turning frequently. Version 1 will take less time, as the ingredients do not need to be cooked but just heated through. Serve at once.

TIP If cooking alongside meat kebabs, be careful that they don't get splattered with fat. And if space on the grill is limited, brush the vegetarian kebabs with oil and cook in the oven instead, watching to make sure they don't overcook.

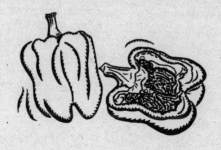

VEGETARIAN CUISINE

Most of the world's population is either completely vegetarian or uses flesh foods as a garnish rather than making them the centrepiece of a meal. Many of the recipes in this chapter are based on traditional vegetarian dishes from around the world, though slight adjustments have been made to compensate for ingredients that are difficult to find. There are also some more original recipes that are part of the new vegetarian cuisine, not imitation meat dishes but specially created to prove that vegetarian food can be exciting in its own right. Serve these dishes to everyone in the family – they are balanced and nutritious and need nothing else added.

You can also, of course, create your own vegetarian dishes. It's much easier than you think, and it can be fun too. It's important to include a grain or starch ingredient, some vegetables and protein, but apart from that, anything goes. Why not a vegetable base with a savoury crumble topping instead of pastry? How about wrapping your favourite lentil mix in filo pastry? Making a sauce with ground nuts? Frying potatoes with spices then serving them with cucumber in yogurt?

Mushroom Tacos

You can buy taco shells all ready to stuff in whatever way you fancy, and their crisp, spicy flavour goes well with an amazing number of fillings, so do be adventurous. The filling given here is not traditionally Mexican, but it's delicious. Try them too with Refried Aduki Beans (page 132) and Chili Non Carne (page 86).

Preparation time: 10 minutes
Cooking time: 10 minutes

METRIC/IMPERIAL	AMERICAN
2 tablespoons vegetable oil	2 tablespoons vegetable oil
1 onion, sliced	1 onion, sliced
1 clove garlic, crushed	1 clove garlic, crushed
1 stick celery, chopped	1 stick celery, chopped
455g/1 lb mushrooms, chopped	8 cups mushrooms, chopped
2 tablespoons chopped fresh parsley	2 tablespoons chopped fresh parsley
seasoning to taste	seasoning to taste
55g/2 oz walnut pieces	½ cup walnut pieces
8 tablespoons soured cream	8 tablespoons soured cream
8 taco shells	8 taco shells
8 cherry tomatoes, quartered	8 cherry tomatoes, quartered
55g/2 oz Cheddar cheese, grated	½ cup grated Cheddar cheese
shredded Iceberg lettuce	shredded Iceberg lettuce

1 Heat the oil in a pan, add the onion, garlic and celery, and cook for 5 minutes until softened. Add the mushrooms and cook for 5 minutes more, or until tender.
2 Drain any excess liquid from the pan, then stir in the parsley, seasoning, walnut pieces and soured cream. Remove from the heat but keep warm.
3 Heat the oven to 200°C/400°F (Gas Mark 6) and lay the taco shells directly on the oven shelves. Leave to heat through for just a few minutes.
4 Pile the warm filling into the shells, top each one with 4 tomato quarters, some grated cheese and some shredded lettuce. Serve at once. They make a good light meal following a starter such as soup and accompanied by a salad.

TIP Though taco shells keep for ages if well wrapped, once you have heated them they are best eaten straight away. If any are left over, you could crumble them over a vegetable dish such as cauliflower cheese. They're also good sprinkled over soups and salads in place of croûtons.

Refried Aduki Beans

Refried beans are so called because they are cooked once, then mashed and cooked again. This recipe cheats – firstly by using ready-cooked beans, and secondly by suggesting aduki beans instead of the more traditional Mexican pinto or black beans. It'll taste almost as good, though! If you want your dish to be more authentic, you know what to do.

Preparation time: 5 minutes
Cooking time: 15 minutes

METRIC/IMPERIAL	AMERICAN
395g/14oz can aduki beans	medium can aduki beans
2 tablespoons vegetable oil	2 tablespoons vegetable oil
1 large onion, finely chopped	1 large onion, finely chopped
1 clove garlic, crushed	1 clove garlic, crushed
2 tablespoons tomato paste	2 tablespoons tomato paste
1 teaspoon chilli powder	1 teaspoon chilli powder
1 teaspoon dried oregano	1 teaspoon dried oregano
seasoning to taste	seasoning to taste
fresh parsley sprigs to garnish	fresh parsley sprigs to garnish
plain yogurt, soured cream or sliced avocado to serve	plain yogurt, soured cream or sliced avocado to serve

1 Drain the beans and mash them coarsely.
2 In a frying pan, heat the oil and add the onion and garlic. Cook until softened, then add the tomato paste, chilli powder, oregano and seasoning. Stir, and cook a minute longer.
3 Add the beans and mix well. Cook gently for 10 minutes more, adding a little water or vegetable stock if the mixture gets too dry – it should be a thick purée.
4 Serve hot, sprinkled generously with parsley sprigs. Delicious topped with yogurt, soured cream or avocado slices. Refried beans could accompany a rice dish, be used to fill pancakes or tacos, or could even be spread over a pizza and heated through.

TIP If you cook this dish a day before you need it, just reheat it gently when you're ready to eat; you'll find the flavour even richer. Vegans could use soya yogurt as a topping.

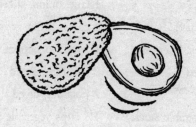

Vegetable Couscous

Couscous is a quick-cooking coarsely ground semolina made from wheat or millet. Traditionally it is served with meat and vegetables which are cooked in a big pot, the couscous being placed on top so that the steam not only softens but flavours it.

Preparation time: 10 minutes (plus soaking time)
Cooking time: 40 minutes

METRIC/IMPERIAL	AMERICAN
455g/1 lb couscous	2 cups couscous
55g/2 oz raisins	⅓ cup raisins
570ml/1 pint boiling water	2½ cups boiling water
2 tablespoons vegetable oil	2 tablespoons vegetable oil
1 large onion, sliced	1 large onion, sliced
2 cloves garlic, crushed	2 cloves garlic, crushed
1 large red pepper, chopped	1 large red pepper, chopped
2 courgettes, sliced	2 zucchini, sliced
2 potatoes, diced	2 potatoes, diced
570ml/1 pint vegetable stock	1½ cups vegetable stock
395g/14 oz can okra, drained	medium can okra, drained
395g/14 oz can chick peas, drained	medium can garbanzo beans, drained
395g/14 oz can tomatoes, chopped	medium can tomatoes, chopped
1 teaspoon ground cumin	1 teaspoon ground cumin
1 teaspoon cayenne pepper	1 teaspoon cayenne pepper
seasoning to taste	seasoning to taste

3 free-range eggs, hard-boiled and quartered	3 free-range eggs, hard-boiled and quartered

1 Put the couscous and raisins into a bowl, pour on the boiling water, cover and leave for 30 minutes, stirring occasionally.
2 Meanwhile, heat the oil in a large saucepan and gently fry the onion, garlic and red pepper for 5 minutes. Add the courgettes (zucchini) and potatoes, pour on the stock and bring to the boil then lower the heat, cover the pan, and cook for 10 minutes. Stir in the okra, chick peas (garbanzo beans), tomatoes, spices and seasoning. Add water if necessary to cover.
3 Transfer the couscous and raisins to the top of a steamer pot (or sieve), first lining it with muslin. Stand this over the vegetables in the pan, cover tightly, and continue simmering the vegetables for about 20 minutes – the steam will cook the couscous.
4 Fluff up the cooked grains and transfer to a serving dish, then top with the vegetable stew. Garnish with the hard-boiled eggs and serve at once.

TIP Other vegetables can be used, including marrow and pumpkin, carrots, aubergine – whatever you prefer.

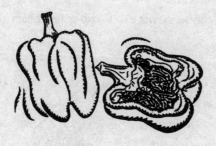

Wheat Berry and Lentil Bake

Cheap, filling, and unusual. Wheat berries make a chewy alternative to rice, bulgur and other grains. Any leftovers can be served cold as a salad – add greens, maybe some tofu or hard-boiled eggs, and a good French dressing.

Preparation time: 10 minutes (plus soaking time)
Cooking time: 1½ hours

METRIC/IMPERIAL	AMERICAN
115g/4 oz wheat berries	½ cup wheat berries
115g/4 oz green lentils, soaked for at least 1 hour	½ cup green lentils, soaked for at least 1 hour
2 leeks, sliced	2 leeks, sliced
2 carrots, sliced	2 carrots, sliced
2 tablespoons vegetable oil	2 tablespoons vegetable oil
30g/1 oz wholemeal flour	¼ cup wholewheat flour
285ml/½ pint milk	1½ cups milk
½ teaspoon ground nutmeg	½ teaspoon ground nutmeg
seasoning to taste	seasoning to taste
85g/3 oz Edam cheese, grated	¾ cup grated Edam cheese

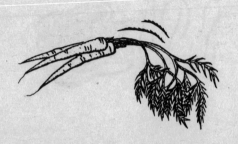

1 Cook the wheat berries in a pan of boiling water for 50 minutes or until just tender, then drain.
2 At the same time, cook the lentils in another pan of water – they should be soft in about 30 minutes. Drain well.
3 Steam the leeks and carrots for 10 minutes.
4 Make a white sauce by heating the oil, stirring in the flour and cooking briefly, then adding the milk. Continue cooking until the sauce thickens, then flavour with the nutmeg and seasoning to taste. Stir in the carrots and leeks.
5 Layer half the wheat berries, lentils and sauce in a greased medium-sized ovenproof dish, then repeat to use all the ingredients. Top with the grated cheese.
6 Bake in the oven at 200°C/400°F (Gas Mark 6) for 30 minutes, or until heated through. Serve at once, with a large crisp salad sprinkled with nuts if you like.

TIP Cooked wheat berries and lentils can both be frozen, so it's worth cooking more than you need and keeping the extra for use another time. Vegans can make the white sauce with soya milk, and top the bake with breadcrumbs and seeds.

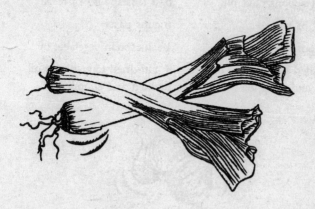

Pasta with Pesto and Sun-Dried Tomatoes

This is another of those simple yet absolutely delicious dishes that can be put together in minutes, especially if you make up a good amount of pesto sauce in advance and keep it in the fridge. Any type of pasta can be used.

Preparation time: 10 minutes
Cooking time: 10 minutes

METRIC/IMPERIAL	AMERICAN
55g/2 oz basil leaves, plus extra to garnish	2 ounces basil leaves, plus extra to garnish
2 cloves garlic, crushed	2 cloves garlic, crushed
30g/1 oz pine nuts	3 tablespoons pine nuts
55g/2 oz Parmesan cheese, freshly grated, plus extra to serve	½ cup freshly grated Parmesan cheese, plus extra to serve
seasoning to taste	seasoning to taste
6–8 tablespoons olive oil	6–8 tablespoons olive oil
340g/12 oz pasta	6 cups pasta
1 tablespoon vegetable oil	1 tablespoon vegetable oil
4 sun-dried tomatoes in oil, drained and chopped	4 sun-dried tomatoes in oil, drained and chopped

1 To make the pesto, combine the basil leaves, garlic, pine nuts, Parmesan cheese and seasoning in a blender. Gradually add the olive oil, a few spoonfuls at a time, until the sauce is smooth and fairly thick.
2 Bring a large pan of water to the boil, add the vegetable oil, then the pasta and cook for about 8 minutes. Drain well.
3 Return the pasta to the pan with the sun-dried tomatoes. Stir in most of the pesto sauce and taste, adding more sauce if necessary. Adding a drop of the pasta cooking water to the sauce will warm it, if you prefer. Pile on to a serving dish and sprinkle with Parmesan cheese and shredded basil leaves. Serve at once..

TIP Pesto can also be used in casseroles, soups, or as a topping for jacket potatoes. Vegans can omit the cheese. In an emergency – or if you don't have a blender – try one of the many excellent ready-made pesto sauces now in the shops.

Beetroot Au Gratin

A satisfying and surprisingly good dish for the beetroot fan in the family.

Preparation time: 10 minutes
Cooking time: 10 minutes

METRIC/IMPERIAL	AMERICAN
680g/1½ lb cooked beetroot	1½ pounds cooked beets
55g/2 oz margarine	¼ cup margarine
55g/2 oz wholemeal flour	½ cup wholewheat flour
425ml/¾ pint milk	2 cups milk
115g/4 oz Cheddar cheese, grated	1 cup grated Cheddar cheese
seasoning to taste	seasoning to taste
2 tablespoons chopped fresh chives	2 tablespoons chopped fresh chives
55g/2 oz walnut pieces	½ cup walnut pieces
30g/1 oz wholemeal breadcrumbs	½ cup wholewheat breadcrumbs
1–2 teaspoons caraway seeds (optional)	1–2 teaspoons caraway seeds (optional)
fresh parsley to garnish	fresh parsley to garnish

1 Peel the beetroot (beets) and cut into cubes. Melt half the margarine in a pan and fry the beetroot (beets) gently, stirring frequently, to heat through.
2 Make the sauce: melt the remaining margarine in a separate pan, add the flour and cook briefly, then stir in the milk. Cook gently until the sauce thickens, then add most of the grated cheese, season well and add the chives.
3 Gently stir the beetroot (beets) into the cheese sauce with the walnut pieces. Transfer to a heatproof dish, sprinkle the top with the remaining cheese and the breadcrumbs, and put under a hot grill (broiler) for a few minutes. Sprinkle with the caraway seeds, if using, and serve garnished with parsley. To complete the meal, serve with a grain such as rice, bulgur or kasha. Kasha is as popular as beetroot in Russia, where the two are often combined.

TIP An even quicker version can be made by mixing the beetroot into soured cream instead of making a white sauce. Stir a little flour into this before heating to stop it curdling. Or to make it into a more filling dish, add a crumble topping.

Mutta Paneer (Cheese and Pea Curry)

This authentic Indian curry uses paneer, a mild cheese that soaks up other flavours, making it especially suitable in spiced dishes such as this. Look out for it in speciality stores and wholefood shops. Vegans can use cubes of tofu instead of the paneer. It has a surprisingly similar texture.

Preparation time: 5 minutes
Cooking time: 30 minutes

METRIC/IMPERIAL	AMERICAN
3 tablespoons ghee (see Tip below) or vegetable oil	3 tablespoons ghee (see Tip below) or vegetable oil
225g/8 oz paneer, diced	1 cup paneer, diced
2 onions, sliced	2 onions, sliced
2 cloves garlic, crushed	2 cloves garlic, crushed
1 tablespoon grated ginger root	1 tablespoon grated ginger root
1 teaspoon turmeric	1 teaspoon turmeric
1 teaspoon ground coriander	1 teaspoon ground coriander
½ teaspoon chilli powder	½ teaspoon chilli powder
225g/8 oz shelled peas or 170g/6 oz frozen peas	½ pound shelled peas or 1 cup frozen peas
3 tomatoes, peeled and chopped	3 tomatoes, peeled and chopped
200ml/⅓ pint water	¾ cup water
garam masala and chopped fresh coriander leaves to garnish	garam masala and chopped fresh coriander leaves to garnish

1 Melt the ghee in a pan, add the paneer and fry for a few minutes until lightly coloured on all sides. Remove with a slotted spoon and keep warm.

2 Add the onions, garlic and ginger to the pan and cook for 5 minutes. Add the spices and cook for a few minutes more.

3 Stir in the peas, tomatoes and water, bring to a boil, then lower the heat and simmer for 15 minutes. Add the paneer and cook for 5 minutes more. Watch that the sauce doesn't boil dry.

4 Transfer the curry to a serving dish and sprinkle with the garam masala and coriander. Serve with rice and/or Indian breads, such as crisp poppadums, or soft warm chapatis.

TIP Ghee is a clarified fat, made from butter or vegetable oil, which is often used in curries. Look out for it in wholefood or speciality shops. When using fresh ginger root, break off a small piece at a time, use a sharp knife to peel off the skin, then rub it against the fine or coarse side of a cheese grater until you have the amount needed. If you find you've grated more than you need, you can freeze the extra. Keep the rest of the root in the fridge.

Mixed Vegetable Curry with Coconut Sauce

V+

Try this on anyone who thinks curries can't be subtle. Mildly flavoured, deliciously coconutty and pretty to look at, it is based on ingredients with which you're probably already familiar.

Preparation time: 5 minutes
Cooking time: 15 minutes

METRIC/IMPERIAL	AMERICAN
2 tablespoons vegetable oil	2 tablespoons vegetable oil
1 large onion, sliced	1 large onion, sliced
1 teaspoon turmeric	1 teaspoon turmeric
1 small cauliflower, broken into florets	1 small cauliflower, broken into florets
225g/8 oz frozen leaf spinach, defrosted	½ pound frozen leaf spinach, defrosted
85g/3 oz split red lentils	⅓ cup split red lentils
285ml/½ pint vegetable stock	1½ cups vegetable stock
115g/4 oz creamed coconut (see Tip below)	½ cup creamed coconut (see Tip below)
1 tablespoon mild curry paste, or to taste	1 tablespoon mild curry paste, or to taste
toasted desiccated coconut to garnish	toasted shredded coconut to garnish
2 tomatoes, quartered	2 tomatoes, quartered

1 Heat the oil in a pan, add the onion and cook for 5 minutes until softened. Stir in the turmeric.
2 Stir in the cauliflower florets, spinach and lentils. Pour in the vegetable stock, bring to a boil, then cook gently for 5 minutes. Break up or grate the creamed coconut and add to the pan with the curry paste. Cook for 5 minutes more.
3 Serve garnished with the toasted coconut and tomato wedges. Good with rice or, for a change, couscous.

TIP Creamed coconut can be bought in supermarkets as well as speciality and wholefood shops. It comes in a block; use a sharp knife or cheese grater to break it up and it will dissolve almost instantly. You can also mix it with a little hot water, sugar and spices to make a delicious vegan 'cream' for topping fruit salads, sweets, crumbles, etc.

Aubergine (Eggplant) and Feta Filo Pie

A pie that will bring back memories of holidays in Greece. Filo
pastry is now widely available – look for it in the chiller cabinet
at your local supermarket or wholefood shop. Though it may seem
complicated to use, you'll soon get the knack (most packs come
with instructions). As you'll be working with only a sheet at a time,
do remember to cover the rest with a damp cloth to keep it from
drying out, which would make the pie topping brittle.

Preparation time: 15 minutes (plus salting the aubergine (eggplant))
Cooking time: 40 minutes

METRIC/IMPERIAL	AMERICAN
1 large aubergine, cut into thick slices	1 large eggplant, cut into thick slices
2 tablespoons vegetable oil, plus extra for brushing filo pastry	2 tablespoons vegetable oil, plus extra for brushing filo pastry
1 large onion, sliced	1 large onion, sliced
1 clove garlic, crushed	1 clove garlic, crushed
395g/14 oz can tomatoes, chopped	medium can tomatoes, chopped
2 tablespoons tomato paste	2 tablespoons tomato paste
½ teaspoon dried thyme	½ teaspoon dried thyme
seasoning to taste	seasoning to taste
115g/4 oz feta cheese, crumbled	1 cup crumbled feta cheese
225g/8 oz cottage cheese	1 cup cottage cheese
55g/2 oz wholemeal breadcrumbs	1 cup wholewheat breadcrumbs
2 tablespoons sesame seeds	2 tablespoons sesame seeds
6 sheets filo pastry, defrosted if necessary	6 sheets filo pastry, defrosted if necessary
vegetable oil	vegetable oil

1 Lay the aubergine (eggplant) slices in a colander, sprinkle with salt and leave for 30 minutes. Then rinse with cold water and pat dry before cutting into cubes.
2 Heat the oil in a frying pan and fry the onion and garlic for 5 minutes until softened. Stir in the aubergine (eggplant) cubes and cook, stirring, a few minutes more. Add the tomatoes, tomato paste, thyme and seasoning, cover, and cook for 10 minutes or until the aubergine (eggplant) is tender.
3 Lightly grease a medium-sized ovenproof dish. Put half the aubergine (eggplant) and tomato mixture in it, top with half the crumbled feta cheese, half the cottage cheese and half the crumbs and sesame seeds. Repeat these layers once more.
4 Unroll a sheet of filo pastry on a lightly floured surface. Brush with oil, then lay it over the pie filling, making sure it comes right to the edge of the dish. Repeat until all but one sheet of the pastry has been used. Cut the last sheet into squares and scrunch them lightly in your hand before arranging them over the top of the pie, again brushing well with oil.
5 Bake the pie in the oven at 190°C/375°F (Gas Mark 5) for 20 minutes, or until the top is crisp and golden. Serve at once with potatoes and a green vegetable or salad.

TIP Vegans can make this pie with hummus instead of the cheese, perhaps adding some coarsely crushed chick peas for texture.

Jacket Potatoes with Fillings

Once jacket potatoes were little more than something to fill a corner of the plate. Nowadays they are served in pubs and cafés across the country as a snack, with a variety of fillings to suit everyone. Instead of serving them with cheese why not try stir-fried vegetables with tofu, ratatouille with walnuts, baked beans (add soya 'bacon' bits for interest), coleslaw with sunflower seeds, curried vegetables . . . The list is endless. You can make them into a meal by serving three halves per person, plus a selection of fillings from which everyone can help themselves. Add a big crisp salad and your meal will be complete.

Below is a basic method for baking jacket potatoes, followed by ideas for fillings.

4 large potatoes, scrubbed and dried
vegetable oil
coarse salt

Brush the potatoes with oil, sprinkle with salt and wrap each one in foil. Bake at 200°C/400°F (Gas Mark 6) for 1–1½ hours. To check if they are cooked, take one in a tea towel and press gently – it should give a little. Cut a cross in the potatoes or halve them, and serve.

TIP When choosing potatoes for baking, look for even-sized, well-shaped ones with no blemishes. The best are old (maincrop) potatoes with a floury texture – try Golden Wonder, Maris Piper and King Edward. You can cut the cooking time by 10–15 minutes if you put a metal skewer through the centre of each potato.

Chilli Avocado Filling

V+

Preparation time: 5 minutes
Cooking time: 15 minutes (plus 1–1½ hours for baking the potatoes)

METRIC/IMPERIAL	AMERICAN
2 tablespoons vegetable oil	2 tablespoons vegetable oil
1 small onion, sliced	1 small onion, sliced
55g/2 oz cooked sweetcorn kernels	⅓ cup cooked corn kernels
200g/7 oz can tomatoes, chopped	small can tomatoes, chopped
1 tablespoon tomato paste	1 tablespoon tomato paste
½ teaspoon chilli powder	½ teaspoon chilli powder
seasoning to taste	seasoning to taste
2 medium avocados, peeled, stoned and chopped	2 medium avocados, peeled pitted and chopped

1 When the potatoes are nearly cooked, heat the oil in a small pan and gently fry the onion for a few minutes. Add the drained sweetcorn, tomatoes, tomato paste, chilli powder and seasoning and simmer for 10 minutes. Stir in the avocado chunks.
2 Pile some of the filling into each of the prepared potatoes. Serve at once.

Broccoli Amandine Filling

Preparation time: 5 minutes
Cooking time: 10–20 minutes
(plus 1–1½ hours for baking the potatoes)

METRIC/IMPERIAL	AMERICAN
225g/8 oz broccoli, trimmed and divided into florets	½ pound broccoli, trimmed and divided into florets
30g/1 oz margarine	2 tablespoons margarine
45g/1½ oz flaked almonds	⅓ cup slivered almonds
squeeze of lemon juice	squeeze of lemon juice
seasoning to taste	seasoning to taste
55g/2 oz Parmesan cheese, grated	½ cup grated Parmesan cheese

1 When the potatoes are nearly cooked, drop the broccoli into a pan of boiling water and cook for 10 minutes or until just tender.
2 Meanwhile, melt the margarine in a small pan and lightly fry the almonds, turning frequently, until they begin to colour. Add the lemon juice and seasoning, stir in the broccoli and cook for just a minute to heat through.
3 Spoon some of the mixture into each of the prepared potatoes, pressing it down, then sprinkle with the Parmesan cheese. Return the filled potato halves to the oven for 10 minutes to brown the tops, or brown them under a hot grill (broiler).

Cheese Soufflé Jacket Potatoes

Preparation time: 10 minutes
Cooking time: 15 minutes (plus 1–1½ hours for baking the potatoes)

METRIC/IMPERIAL	AMERICAN
2 free-range eggs, separated	2 free-range eggs, separated
85g/3 oz Red Leicester or Cheddar cheese, grated	¾ cup grated Red Leicester or Cheddar cheese
85g/3 oz cottage cheese	⅓ cup cottage cheese
1 tablespoon chopped fresh chives	1 tablespoon chopped fresh chives
seasoning to taste	seasoning to taste
watercress to garnish	watercress to garnish

1 When the potatoes are cooked, halve them then use a spoon to scoop out most of the flesh. Put this into a bowl and mash with the egg yolks, Red Leicester and cheese and cottage cheese, chives and seasoning.
2 Whisk the egg whites until stiff, then fold them into the potato mixture. Spoon this into the potato skins, piling it high. Return to the oven and bake for about 15 minutes, or until well risen. Serve garnished with watercress.

Vegetable and Cashew Stir-Fry

V+

Though the stir-fry method of cooking has been around for thousands of years it could have been designed for today's busy cooks. No other dish takes so little time to prepare or cook, is so healthy, so versatile – and results in such a variety of delicious tastes. Do invest in a wok – it makes stir-frying so much easier.

Preparation time: 10 minutes
Cooking time: 10 minutes

METRIC/IMPERIAL	AMERICAN
3 tablespoons vegetable oil	3 tablespoons vegetable oil
1 teaspoon grated fresh ginger	1 teaspoon grated fresh ginger
115g/4 oz button mushrooms, sliced	2 cups sliced button mushrooms
2 carrots, thinly sliced	2 carrots, thinly sliced
¼ small white cabbage, sliced	¼ small white cabbage, sliced
115g/4 oz mangetout	¼ pound snow peas
1 tablespoon soy sauce	1 tablespoon soy sauce
1 tablespoon dry sherry	1 tablespoon dry sherry
1 tablespoon raw cane sugar	1 tablespoon raw cane sugar
85g/3 oz cashew halves	⅔ cup cashew halves

1 Heat the oil in a wok or large frying pan, add the ginger and mushrooms and stir-fry for 1 minute. Add the carrots, cabbage and mangetout and continue stir-frying over a medium heat for another 5 minutes.

2 Mix together the soy sauce, sherry and sugar. Pour this over the vegetables, stir in the nuts, then cook for a further 3–4 minutes.

3 Serve at once with fried rice or noodles (you can stir the cooked rice in with the vegetables and heat it through briefly if you like). Another excellent accompaniment would be Beansprout Spring Rolls (see below).

TIP Any vegetables can be stir-fried in a similar way. You can add garlic and onion if you like, or use cornflour (cornstarch) and vegetable stock to make a thicker sauce. Sweet and sour sauces also go well with stir-fried vegetables. Always make sure you have all the vegetables prepared before you start cooking, and that they are cut into similar-sized pieces. Think about the appearance of the dish, too. Carrots, baby corn, celery, etc, all look attractive cut diagonally.

Bean Sprout Spring Rolls

❖

V+

Light and crispy, with a crunchy, fresh-tasting vegetable filling, these rolls are surprisingly easy to make.

Preparation time: 15 minutes
Cooking time: 30 minutes

METRIC/IMPERIAL	AMERICAN
1 tablespoon vegetable oil, plus extra for brushing filo pastry	1 tablespoon vegetable oil, plus extra for brushing filo pastry
1 small onion, chopped	1 small onion, chopped
1 carrot, chopped	1 carrot, chopped
55g/2 oz mushrooms, coarsely chopped	1 cup mushrooms, coarsely chopped
3 tablespoons cooked sweetcorn kernels	3 tablespoons cooked corn kernels
55g/2 oz mung bean sprouts	1 cup mung bean sprouts
200g/7 oz can tomatoes, chopped	small can tomatoes, chopped
seasoning to taste	seasoning to taste
6 sheets filo pastry, defrosted if frozen	6 sheets filo pastry, defrosted if frozen
watercress to garnish	watercress to garnish

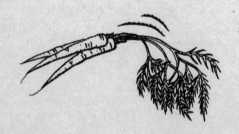

1 Heat the oil in a pan and gently fry the onion and carrot until softened. Stir in the mushrooms and cook briefly, then add the sweetcorn, bean sprouts, tomatoes and seasoning and heat through for 5 more minutes. Season generously.

2 Unroll one sheet of filo pastry on a board, then cut it in half so you have 2 pieces about 18cm/7 in square (leave the other sheets well wrapped while you work, to prevent them drying). Brush each square lightly with oil, put a spoonful of the bean sprout mixture in the centre, fold a little pastry over the filling at each side, then roll up loosely. Brush the top with more oil, then transfer the roll carefully to a baking sheet. Repeat with the remaining pastry and filling to make 12 rolls.

3 Bake the rolls in the oven at 200°C/400°F (Gas Mark 6) for about 15 minutes, or until lightly browned. You may need to turn them over.

4 Serve garnished with watercress. As a main meal they can be accompanied by rice, or maybe bulgur or millet for a change.

TIP Though filo pastry needs to be handled with care, it is easy to use once you have had a little practice – and usually produces very impressive results. If, however, you have doubts, these spring rolls can be made using small, thin pancakes instead of the pastry, or even puff pastry.

Gnocchi with Tomato and Garlic Sauce

If you've only eaten semolina as a stodgy, over-sweet pudding, here's a chance to try something completely different. A simple, inexpensive dish, gnocchi is popular throughout Italy.

Preparation time: 10 minutes (plus infusing time)
Cooking time: 40 minutes

METRIC/IMPERIAL	AMERICAN
1 onion, chopped	1 onion, chopped
1 bay leaf	1 bay leaf
570ml/1 pint milk	2½ cups milk
115g/4 oz wholemeal semolina	1 cup wholewheat semolina
30g/1 oz margarine	2 tablespoons margarine
55g/2 oz Parmesan cheese, grated	½ cup grated Parmesan cheese
1 teaspoon mustard	1 teaspoon mustard
seasoning to taste	seasoning to taste
fresh parsley to garnish	fresh parsley to garnish

For the sauce

1 tablespoon vegetable oil	1 tablespoon vegetable oil
1 onion, chopped	1 onion, chopped
2 cloves garlic, crushed	2 cloves garlic, crushed
395g/14 oz can tomatoes, chopped	1 medium can tomatoes, chopped
seasoning to taste	seasoning to taste
2 tablespoons chopped fresh parsley, plus extra to garnish	2 tablespoons chopped fresh parsley, plus extra to garnish
2–4 tablespoons soured cream or soft cheese	2–4 tablespoons soured cream or soft cheese

1 Put the onion and bay leaf into a saucepan with the milk, bring to a boil, then remove from the heat, cover and leave for 30 minutes to infuse. Strain the milk, discarding the onion and bay leaf.

2 In a clean pan, heat the milk and sprinkle in the semolina. Cook, stirring, for a few minutes until the mixture thickens, then add the margarine, cheese, mustard and seasoning. Wet a Swiss roll tin (jelly roll pan), pour off any excess water, then spoon in the semolina mixture and smooth the top. Chill briefly.

3 To make the sauce, simply combine all the ingredients except the soured cream or soft cheese in a saucepan, bring to a boil, then cover and simmer for 15 minutes. Cool slightly then blend to make a completely smooth sauce. Stir in the soured cream or soft cheese.

4 Use a small glass or cutter to cut the semolina into rounds. Arrange these, overlapping slightly, in a greased ovenproof dish. Pour on the sauce.

5 Bake in the oven at 200°C/400°F (Gas Mark 6) for 15 minutes. Serve at once, garnished with lots of parsley.

TIP If you don't have a Swiss roll tin (jelly roll pan), just roll the semolina paste out on a board to a thickness of about 2.5cm/1 in and leave to set. You can prepare the gnocchi mixture a day in advance and leave it in the fridge, adding the sauce just before you put it into the oven to heat through. You can also sprinkle over cheese, walnut pieces, breadcrumbs, poppy seeds – whatever you like – to give the dish a special topping.

Pan Haggarty

A simple dish which gives potatoes a whole new image. This version includes parsnips, and is one of the tastiest ways of eating this much-overlooked vegetable.

Preparation time: 10 minutes
Cooking time: 30 minutes

METRIC/IMPERIAL	AMERICAN
680g/1½ lb new potatoes, thinly sliced	1½ pounds new potatoes, thinly sliced
225g/8 oz young parsnips, thinly sliced	½ pound young parsnips, thinly sliced
30g/1 oz margarine	2 tablespoons margarine
1 tablespoon vegetable oil	1 tablespoon vegetable oil
2 onions, sliced	2 onions, sliced
170g/6 oz Edam cheese, grated	1½ cups grated Edam cheese
seasoning to taste	seasoning to taste

1 Bring a large saucepan of water to the boil and cook the potatoes and parsnips in it for just 2 minutes. Drain and rinse under cold water, then dry well.

2 Combine the margarine and oil in a large frying pan and heat gently. Add the onions and fry for 5 minutes until softened, then use a slotted spoon to remove them, leaving as much of the fat as possible in the pan.

3 Cover the base of the frying pan with rings of potato and parsnip slices, using about half. Spread half the onions over them, then half the grated cheese and seasoning. Repeat these layers once more to use the remaining ingredients.

4 Cover the pan and cook over a low heat for 20 minutes, then remove the lid and put the pan under a hot grill (broiler) for a few minutes to brown the top. Serve hot, cut into generous wedges. Good accompaniments would be hot stewed tomatoes and a green vegetable such as spinach, sprinkled with nuts.

TIP If you don't have a frying pan with a lid, use silver foil instead. Ring the changes by using turnips instead of parsnips, and try other cheeses such as smoked Cheddar, or a herbed cheese.

Fondue

What better way to share a meal with family or friends? This is worth buying a fondue set for, especially if it becomes a regular dish in your house, though you can make do with a casserole or heavy-based saucepan if necessary.

Preparation time: 15 minutes
Cooking time: 15 minutes

METRIC/IMPERIAL	AMERICAN
15g/½ oz margarine	1 tablespoon margarine
285ml/½ pint light ale	1⅓ cups light ale
1 teaspoon lemon juice	1 teaspoon lemon juice
455g/1 lb Gruyère cheese, grated	4 cups grated Gruyère cheese
½ teaspoon ground mixed spice	½ teaspoon ground mixed spice
seasoning to taste	seasoning to taste
1 tablespoon arrowroot	1 tablespoon potato starch
2 tablespoons cold water	2 tablespoons cold water

Accompaniments	Accompaniments
wholemeal bread, cubed	wholewheat bread, cubed
croûtons	croûtons
tortilla chips	tortilla chips
chunks of apple and pear	chunks of apple and pear
raw vegetables, e.g. button mushrooms, carrot and celery sticks, radishes, courgettes	raw vegetables, e.g. button mushrooms, carrot and celery sticks, radishes, zucchini
small, lightly cooked new potatoes	small, lightly cooked new potatoes

1 Use the margarine to grease the sides and base of a fondue pan or a casserole dish or heavy-based saucepan.

2 Pour in the light ale and lemon juice and heat gently, then add the cheese, stirring until it has melted. Add the mixed spice and seasoning.

3 In a small bowl blend together the arrowroot (potato starch) and cold water. Mix this into the cheese and continue heating until the sauce thickens.

4 Take the pan to the table, if possible standing it over a candle burner to keep it warm and also to stop the mixture becoming too thick. Serve with an assortment of attractively presented accompaniments to be dipped into it, plus some long forks to make the task less difficult. The idea is that everyone simply helps themselves.

TIP If the fondue is to be the main course of your meal, start with a crunchy salad. You can use dry white wine or cider instead of the light ale or, if you prefer to avoid alcohol, vegetable stock. Try making your fondue with different cheeses, too, and flavouring it with tomato paste or curry powder – whatever you fancy.

Hazelnut Pancakes Peperonata

V+

The slightly heavy texture of these eggless pancakes is compensated for by the moist, flavourful filling.

Preparation time: 20 minutes (plus standing time for batter)
Cooking time: 50–60 minutes

METRIC/IMPERIAL

For the pancakes

115g/4 oz wholemeal flour

55g/2 oz soya flour

2 teaspoons baking powder

1 tablespoon coarsely ground toasted hazelnuts

285ml/½ pint water, or soya milk and water mixed

2 tablespoons vegetable oil, plus extra for frying

For the filling

3 tablespoons vegetable oil

1 large onion, sliced

1–2 cloves garlic, crushed

1 bay leaf

1 large green pepper, sliced

1 large red pepper, sliced

1 large yellow pepper, sliced

seasoning to taste

115g/4 oz tofu, drained

chopped fresh parsley to garnish

55g/2 oz vegan margarine (optional)

AMERICAN

For the pancakes

1 cup wholewheat flour

½ cup soy flour

2 teaspoons baking powder

1 tablespoon coarsely ground toasted hazelnuts

1¼ cups water, or soya milk and water mixed

2 tablespoons vegetable oil plus extra for frying

For the filling

3 tablespoons vegetable oil

1 large onion, sliced

1–2 cloves garlic, crushed

1 bay leaf

1 large green pepper, sliced

1 large red pepper, sliced

1 large yellow pepper, sliced

seasoning to taste

1 cup tofu, drained

chopped fresh parsley to garnish

¼ cup vegan margarine (optional)

1 To make the pancake batter, mix the flours together in a bowl, add the baking powder and hazelnuts, then gradually add the liquid, stirring continuously to break up any lumps. Whisk energetically, then whisk in the oil. Cover, and leave in a cool place for at least 30 minutes.

2 Meanwhile, make the peperonata filling. Heat the oil in a pan, add the onion, garlic and bay leaf and cook for 5 minutes. Stir in the sliced peppers and cook for a few minutes more, then cover the pan and leave to cook over a low heat for about 30 minutes, stirring occasionally. Season to taste and remove the bay leaf.

3 Coarsely mash the tofu and stir it into the peperonata. Heat through gently.

4 Before making the pancakes, whisk the batter again and, if necessary, add a drop more liquid. Heat a spoonful of oil in a medium-sized heavy-based frying pan and, when hot, pour in a thin layer of batter, tilting the pan so it spreads to the edges. Cook gently until lightly browned underneath, shaking the pan occasionally to prevent sticking. Toss the pancake or turn it with a spatula and cook the other side. Keep it warm while using the remaining batter in the same way.

5 Divide the peperonata between the pancakes and fold, then serve at once, garnished with parsley. Alternatively, arrange the pancakes in a lightly greased ovenproof dish, dot with the margarine, and bake in the oven at 190°C/375°F (Gas Mark 5) for 10 minutes.

TIP The thinner the batter, the lighter your pancakes will be. How many pancakes you can make from this quantity of batter will vary depending on the thickness of the batter and the size of your pan, though it should make about 8. Any unused pancakes can be frozen individually, then wrapped in foil, stacked, and put back into the freezer. Try replacing half the wholemeal flour with buckwheat flour to make buckwheat pancakes.

Falafels

V+

A classic vegetarian dish from the Middle East where falafels are a popular snack. They are often bought from stalls by hungry locals, who eat them as they walk along the road – rather like our burgers, only much more interesting! This recipe is less spicy than some, but you can, of course, add more garlic, spices, and some chopped onion, if you like your falafel hot.

Preparation time: 15 minutes
Cooking time: 10 minutes

METRIC/IMPERIAL	AMERICAN
395g/14 oz can chick peas	medium can chick peas
55g/2 oz wholemeal breadcrumbs	1 cup wholewheat breadcrumbs
4 tablespoons tahini	4 tablespoons tahini
1 clove garlic, crushed	1 clove garlic, crushed
1 carrot, grated	1 carrot, grated
1 tablespoon chopped fresh parsley	1 tablespoon chopped fresh parsley
½ teaspoon cayenne pepper	½ teaspoon cayenne pepper
½ teaspoon cumin	½ teaspoon cumin
seasoning to taste	seasoning to taste
wholemeal flour	wholemeal flour
vegetable oil for deep-frying	vegetable oil for deep-frying

1 Drain the chick peas, reserving the liquid, then use a grinder or food processor to reduce them to a powder. They can also be broken up using a mortar and pestle, though this is much harder work!

2 In a bowl combine the chick peas, breadcrumbs, tahini, garlic, carrot, parsley, spices and seasoning. Add just a spoonful or two of the liquid from the chick peas to bind the ingredients, then divide the mixture into small pieces and, with floured hands, roll them into balls.

3 Heat the oil in a deep pan and drop in half the falafels, cooking them for 5 minutes or until crisp and golden. Drain on kitchen paper and keep them warm while cooking the rest in the same way. Traditionally falafels are served with hummus (see below), which makes the perfect contrast. For a complete meal, add pita bread or rice and vegetables such as aubergine (eggplant) and peppers or a green salad.

TIP For firmer-textured falafels, add an egg (but not for vegans). If you're intending to serve the falafels cold, at a picnic or as part of a buffet, for example, this will help them hold together. You can also make falafels with different herbs and try replacing some of the chick peas with other beans.

Hummus with Avocado

V+

This is an unusual version of hummus – not that there is anything wrong with the basic hummus, which is a treat just as it is, but it's good to have a change sometimes. If you don't like avocado, replace it with a few spoonfuls of tahini or, for vegetarians, yogurt or soft white cheese.

Preparation time: 10 minutes
Cooking time: None

METRIC/IMPERIAL	AMERICAN
395g/14 oz can chick peas	medium can chick peas
2 tablespoons lemon juice	2 tablespoons lemon juice
2 cloves garlic, crushed	2 cloves garlic, crushed
½–1 teaspoon chilli powder	½–1 tesapoon chilli powder
1 teaspoon ground cumin	1 teaspoon ground cumin
seasoning to taste	seasoning to taste
140ml/¼ pint olive oil	⅔ cup olive oil
2 ripe avocados	2 ripe avocados
2 tablespoons sesame seeds	2 tablespoons sesame seeds
lemon wedges and watercress to garnish	lemon wedges and watercress to garnish

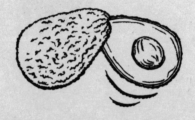

1 Drain the chick peas, reserving the liquid. Put the chick peas,
   lemon juice, garlic, spices and seasoning into a blender or food
   processor and mix well. Gradually add the oil, then add enough
   of the liquid from the chick peas to obtain the consistency you
   prefer. Transfer the mixture to a bowl.

2 Peel, stone and coarsely mash the avocados, then stir them into
   the hummus. Chill briefly. Transfer to an attractive dish and
   serve sprinkled with the sesame seeds and garnished with
   lemon wedges and watercress. Especially good with falafels (see
   above).

*TIP Hummus – whichever version you make – can be used in a variety of
ways. Stir it into soups and casseroles, use it to bind ingredients when stuffing
vegetables or making pasties, or mix it with French dressing and use to dress
a white cabbage salad.*

Fennel and Mozzarella Pizzas

———◆•◆———

You can use this basic recipe as a starting point for making other pizzas.

Preparation time: 25 minutes (plus rising time for dough)
Cooking time: 15–20 minutes

METRIC/IMPERIAL

For the base

200g/7 oz wholemeal flour or half wholemeal, half strong white flour

1 teaspoon Easy-Blend dried yeast

140ml/¼ pint tepid water

1 tablespoon vegetable oil, preferably olive oil

For the topping

395g/14 oz can tomatoes, chopped

1 clove garlic, crushed

1 large fennel bulb, thinly sliced

170g/6 oz mozzarella cheese, sliced

1 red pepper

10 black olives, stoned and halved

10 fresh basil leaves, shredded

55g/2 oz Parmesan cheese, grated

seasoning to taste

vegetable oil, preferably olive oil

AMERICAN

For the base

1¾ cups wholewheat flour or half wholewheat, half all-purpose flour

1 teaspoon Easy-Blend dried yeast

⅔ cup tepid water

1 tablespoon vegetable oil, preferably olive oil

For the topping

medium can tomatoes, chopped

1 clove garlic, crushed

1 large fennel bulb, thinly sliced

1½ cups mozzarella cheese, sliced

1 red pepper

10 black olives, pitted and halved

10 fresh basil leaves, shredded

½ cup grated Parmesan cheese

seasoning to taste

vegetable oil, preferably olive oil

1 Put the flour into a bowl and stir in the yeast. Mix in the water and oil to make a soft dough, then transfer it to a lightly floured board and knead for 5–10 minutes until it is soft and elastic.

2 Put the dough in a clean, floured bowl, cover, and leave in a warm spot for 1 hour or until doubled in size. Knock it back and knead for 3 minutes more. Divide into 4 even-sized pieces, roll into balls, then press out with your hands to make 4 small rounds.

3 Drain the tomatoes and mix well with the garlic, then spread this over the prepared bases. Arrange the fennel slices on top, then half the cheese slices. Cut the red pepper into thin rings and divide these between the pizzas. Top with the rest of the mozzarella slices, then the olives, shredded basil, Parmesan cheese and seasoning. Drizzle a little oil over everything.

4 Bake in the oven at 230°C/450°F (Gas Mark 8) for 15–20 minutes. Serve at once.

TIP The most time-consuming part of making pizza is making the base. Fortunately, it is now possible to buy vacuum-packed ready-made bases, or others that can be kept frozen until needed. Then all you need to do is add the topping of your choice. To make vegan pizzas, use the same basic tomato mixture then add vegetables, nuts, vegan 'cheese' or tofu, plus a drizzle of olive oil, and cook in the same way.

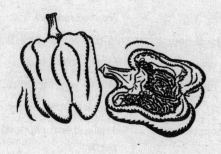

Onion and Pea Oat Crumble

V+

Crumbles needn't only be made with sweet ingredients. Try this smooth, nutty vegetable mixture covered with a crunchy topping, then go on to devise more combinations of your own. This is also an excellent way to turn leftovers into a main dish.

Preparation time: 10 minutes
Cooking time: 40–50 minutes

METRIC/IMPERIAL	AMERICAN
For the filling	**For the filling**
4 large onions, sliced	4 large onions, sliced
170g/6 oz frozen peas	1 cup frozen peas
2 tablespoons vegetable oil	2 tablespoons vegetable oil
30g/1 oz wholemeal flour	¼ cup wholewheat flour
200ml/⅓ pint vegetable stock	¾ cup vegetable stock
55g/2 oz ground almonds	½ cup ground almonds
1 tablespoon soy sauce	1 tablespoon soy sauce
½ teaspoon dried sage, or to taste	½ teaspoon dried sage, or to taste
seasoning to taste	seasoning to taste
For the crumble	**For the crumble**
55g/2 oz wholemeal flour	½ cup wholewheat flour
55g/2 oz rolled oats	½ cup rolled oats
55g/2 oz vegan margarine	¼ cup vegan margarine
30g/1 oz almonds, chopped	3 tablespoons chopped almonds
1 tablespoon chopped fresh parsley	1 tablespoon chopped fresh parsley

1 Cook the onions and peas in a pan of boiling water for 5 minutes, then drain well.

2 Heat the oil in a saucepan, add the flour and cook for a few minutes before pouring in the stock. Heat gently, stirring, until the sauce thickens. Add the ground almonds, soy sauce, sage and seasoning. Mix the sauce with the vegetables, adding a little more liquid if necessary. Transfer to a medium-sized ovenproof dish.

3 Make the crumble by stirring together the flour and oats in a bowl, then using your fingertips to rub in the margarine. Stir in the almonds and parsley and spread the mixture over the onions, smoothing the top and pressing it down lightly.

4 Bake in the oven at 190°C/375°F (Gas Mark 5) for 20–30 minutes, or until the crumble topping is nicely browned. Serve at once.

TIP If you are short of time, use nut butter instead of the sauce, or use tahini for a more subtle taste altogether. Other vegetables could be substituted for the onions and peas. This crumble could be served as an accompaniment to a savoury dish such as burgers, or with rice. It's always worth making up extra crumble mix when you have time and keeping it in an airtight container in the fridge, ready to use for a crumble or, with water added, as pastry.

Chestnut and Leek Tarts

———•◦•———

A classic combination in a new guise. Apart from being delicious served with baby new potatoes and a bitter green salad, these little tarts are very tasty cold.

Preparation time: 30 minutes (plus chilling time)
Cooking time: 30–45 minutes

METRIC/IMPERIAL	AMERICAN
For the pastry	**For the pastry**
115g/4 oz wholemeal flour	1 cup wholewheat flour
55g/2 oz margarine	¼ cup margarine
1 small free-range egg, beaten	1 small free-range egg, beaten
1 tablespon sesame seeds	1 tablespoon sesame seeds
For the filling	**For the filling**
2 medium leeks, cleaned and sliced	2 medium leeks, cleaned and sliced
115g/4 oz chestnuts	4 ounces chestnuts
30g/1 oz margarine	2 tablespoons margarine
30g/1 oz wholemeal flour	¼ cup wholewheat flour
200ml/⅓ pint vegetable stock	¾ cup vegetable stock
85g/3 oz Cheddar cheese, grated	¾ cup grated Cheddar cheese
seasoning to taste	seasoning to taste

1 Put the flour into a bowl, rub in the margarine with your fingertips to make a crumb-like mixture, then add the egg to bind and the sesame seeds. Cover the dough and refrigerate for 30 minutes.

2 Lightly steam the leeks until just tender, then drain well.

3 Cut a cross in the top of each chestnut, drop them into a saucepan of boiling water and cook for 10 minutes. Then use a sharp knife to peel them, removing both the outer and inner skin. If they are still firm, return them to the water and cook for a further 10 minutes or until tender. Drain well and chop coarsely.

4 Melt the margarine in a pan, add the flour and cook for a few minutes before stirring in the stock. Heat gently, stirring, until the mixture thickens. Mix in the leeks, chestnuts, most of the cheese and the seasoning.

5 Roll out the pastry and use to line 4 lightly greased individual flan tins. Divide the filling between them, and top with the remaining cheese. Bake in the oven at 200°C/400°F (Gas Mark 6) for 15–20 minutes. Serve with jacket potatoes and green vegetables.

TIP You can use dried chestnuts instead of fresh ones. Other vegetables can be used instead of the leeks. Vegans can make the pastry without the egg, and mix the leeks and chestnuts with a white sauce made with soya milk, adding plenty of parsley for extra flavour instead of the cheese.

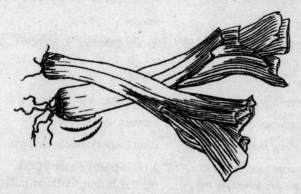

Mixed Stuffed Vegetables

———◆◆◆———

These are a clever way of making a lot of bits and pieces into one wholesome meal. You could serve just one kind of vegetable or you could stuff a trio of vegetables with a single filling. If you really want to impress, try using different vegetables *and* different fillings. Many can be prepared in advance. Note, though, that the ones given in this recipe have been carefully chosen because they take about the same time to cook.

Preparation time: 20 minutes
Cooking time: 40 minutes

METRIC/IMPERIAL	AMERICAN
2 large red peppers	2 large red peppers
2 large onions, peeled	2 large onions, peeled
2 courgettes	2 zucchini

Filling 1	**Filling 1**
1 tablespoon vegetable oil	1 tablespoon vegetable oil
2 tablespoons chopped onion	2 tablespoons chopped onion
4 tablespoons cooked rice	4 tablespoons cooked rice
4 tablespoons cooked peas	4 tablespoons cooked peas
seasoning to taste	seasoning to taste
55g/2 oz feta cheese, crumbled	½ cup crumbled feta cheese

Filling 2	**Filling 2**
2 free-range eggs, hard-boiled	2 free-range eggs, hard-boiled
1 carrot, grated	1 carrot, grated
1 stick celery, finely chopped	1 stick celery, finely chopped
3 tablespoons cooked grain, such as bulgur, kasha or millet	3 tablespoons cooked grain, such as bulgur, kasha or millet

Filling 3

55g/2 oz wholemeal breadcrumbs	1 cup wholewheat breadcrumbs
2 spring onions, chopped	2 scallions, chopped
2 tomatoes, skinned and chopped	2 tomatoes, skinned and chopped
3 tablespoons tahini	3 tablespoons tahini
a few spoonfuls vegetable stock	a few spoonfuls vegetable stock
1 tablespoon chopped fresh parsley	1 tablespoon chopped fresh parsley
seasoning to taste	seasoning to taste
2 tablespoons pumpkin seeds	2 tablespoons pumpkin seeds

1 Bring a large saucepan of water to the boil, add the peppers and cook for 5 minutes. Add the onions and cook for 5 minutes more. Add the courgettes (zucchini) and cook for another 5 minutes. Drain all the vegetables well.

2 When cool, cut the peppers and onions in half crossways, the courgettes (zucchini) lengthways. Cut or scoop out as much of the flesh as possible. Arrange the vegetables on lightly greased baking trays.

3 To prepare the first filling, heat the oil in a frying pan and fry the onion until softened, then stir in the remaining other ingredients. Use it to stuff the pepper halves.

4 To prepare the second filling, chop the hard-boiled eggs and mix them with the remaining ingredients. Pile this mixture into the prepared onion halves.

5 To prepare the third filling, mix together the breadcrumbs, spring onions (scallions) and tomatoes. Mix the tahini with a few spoonfuls of warm vegetable stock, then add· to the breadcrumb mixture with the parsley, seasoning and pumpkin seeds. Use this to stuff the courgettes (zucchini).

6 Bake the stuffed vegetables in the oven at 190°C/375°F (Gas Mark 5) for about 20 minutes. Serve hot or cold.

Millet Pilaff

V+

If you have never eaten millet, try this delicately flavoured pilaff and you'll discover just how easy it is to prepare – and how far just a little goes!

Preparation time: 10 minutes
Cooking time: 25 minutes

METRIC/IMPERIAL	AMERICAN
225g/8 oz millet	1 cup millet
2 tablespoons vegetable oil	2 tablespoons vegetable oil
1 large onion, chopped	1 large onion, chopped
2 cloves garlic, crushed	2 cloves garlic, crushed
1 red pepper, chopped	1 red pepper, chopped
1 stick celery, chopped	1 stick celery, chopped
2.5cm/1 in piece of cinnamon stick	1 inch piece of cinnamon stick
570ml/1 pint vegetable stock	2½ cups vegetable stock
½ teaspoon turmeric	½ teaspon turmeric
½ teaspoon ground cardamom	½ teaspoon ground cardamom
55g/2 oz raisins	⅓ cup raisins
55g/2 oz pistachio nuts	½ cup pistachio nuts
lemon wedges to garnish	lemon wedges to garnish

1 Put the millet into a heavy-based saucepan and dry roast it over a medium heat for a few minutes, then tip it into a bowl and set aside.
2 In the same pan, heat the oil and gently fry the onion, garlic, red pepper and celery for 5 minutes.
3 Add the cinnamon stick, millet, vegetable stock and spices. Bring to a boil then cover the pan, lower the heat, and cook for 10 minutes more. Stir in the raisins.
4 Continue cooking for 5 minutes, or until the millet is cooked and the liquid has been absorbed. Remove the cinnamon stick and, if necessary, drain off any excess liquid. Turn the millet into a warmed serving dish and fluff it up with a fork. Sprinkle with the pistachio nuts and serve at once, garnished with lemon wedges. Serve with a vegetable bake, or with hot falafels (see page 164) and yogurt.

TIP Any leftovers can be shaped into balls or croquettes, with cheese and/or egg added if you like, and then fried. Vary the recipe by using half millet, half rice.

Pakora Vegetables

———————————————

This is an Indian dish of vegetables coated in a batter made with gram flour then deep-fried. When cooked properly, the crunchy, spicy coating makes a perfect contrast to the just-tender vegetables.

Preparation time: 10 minutes (plus chilling time)
Cooking time: 10 minutes

METRIC/IMPERIAL	AMERICAN
For the batter	**For the batter**
225g/8 oz gram flour (see Tip below)	2 cups gram flour (see Tip below)
2 teaspoons ground cumin	2 teaspoons ground cumin
½ teaspoon cayenne pepper	½ teaspoon cayenne pepper
seasoning to taste	seasoning to taste
vegetable oil for deep-frying	vegetable oil for deep-frying
For the vegetables	**For the vegetables**
½ small cauliflower, broken into florets	½ small cauliflower, broken into florets
2 small courgettes, cut into fingers	2 small zucchini, cut into fingers
1 large onion, cut into rings	1 large onion, cut into rings
115g/4 oz button mushrooms	2 cups button mushrooms
1 red pepper, cut into fingers	1 red pepper, cut into fingers
chutneys to serve	chutneys to serve

1 In a bowl mix together the flour, spices and seasoning, then add just enough cold water to make a smooth batter of medium consistency. Chill it for at least an hour.

2 Heat some oil in a deep pan – it is ready if it spits when you drop a little batter into it. Dip the vegetables into the batter a few at a time, making sure they are evenly coated, then drop them into the oil and cook until crisp and well coloured. Drain on paper towels and keep warm while you cook the rest of the vegetables in the same way.

3 Serve hot with a choice of chutneys. For a complete meal, add a rice and nut dish, a tomato salad and perhaps banana slices in yogurt.

TIP Gram flour is made from pulses rather than wheat – usually chick pea. You'll find it in speciality and wholefood shops. Tempura vegetables, which come from the Far East, are prepared in a similar way but use a batter made with wheat flour. Try them for a change, serving them with a dip made from soy sauce, lemon juice and ginger.

Fried Goat's Cheese

Here's a way of serving cheese hot as the protein part of a meal with the minimum of work. A wide variety of cheeses, both firm and soft can be used – Cheddar, Dutch cheeses, mozzarella, Brie and Camembert can be used the same way, or try Haloumi, a Cypriot cheese with a strong salty taste.

Preparation time: 10 minutes
Cooking time: 5 minutes

METRIC/IMPERIAL	AMERICAN
225g/8 oz goat's cheese	½ pound goat's cheese
1 large free-range egg yolk	1 large free-range egg yolk
115g/4 oz dry wholemeal breadcrumbs	2 cups dry wholewheat breadcrumbs
seasoning to taste	seasoning to taste
¼ teaspoon dried basil	¼ teaspoon dried basil
vegetable oil for shallow-frying	vegetable oil for shallow-frying
lemon wedges to serve	lemon wedges to serve

1 If necessary, drain the cheese and pat dry. Cut it into small, even-sized pieces, preferably small rounds or cubes.
2 Lightly beat the egg yolk in one bowl. In another, stir together the breadcrumbs, seasoning and basil.
3 Dip the pieces of cheese into the egg yolk, then into the breadcrumb mixture. Heat the oil in a pan and shallow fry the cheese for about 5 minutes, turning once, until the coating is crisp and golden and the inside soft. Serve at once, garnished with lemon wedges. Particularly good with a dish such as ratatouille, maybe with rice or bulgur. Or serve with potatoes and green vegetables.

TIP *If you don't eat eggs you can make a batter of flour and water to replace the yolk. Have the oil fairly hot and fry the cheese quickly for the best results.*

SWEET TREATS

A chapter on sweet things for vegetarians may seem rather unnecessary. After all, who makes cakes from meat or fish? In fact, there are more animal ingredients than you may realize in puddings and sweets. Suet puddings, for example, are made with animal fat. Jellies are set using gelatine, which is produced by boiling animals' hooves and tendons. Some commercially made yogurts, ice-creams and sweets such as Turkish Delight also contain gelatine, while commercially made cakes and desserts may contain animal fats, and colourings derived from animal sources.

Fortunately, good cruelty-free alternatives are now widely available, : o you can get the same results – if not better – without needing to use any of these ingredients.

There is also another reason for a chapter on sweet treats. There has long been a belief that anything sweet must be bad for you. Switching to a vegetarian diet means considering food as a source of energy and nourishment, but also as a pleasure. And there is no reason at all why this shouldn't apply to desserts, biscuits, cakes and sweets. You can end your meal with a sumptuous pudding, or bridge that mid-afternoon gap with something sweet, or even have muffins for breakfast, knowing that you're doing the right thing for your body as well as your taste buds.

Fig and Kiwi Tarts

V+

These simple little tarts are perfect for a summer tea – especially if you have access to a fig tree. Use figs that are plump and soft, wiping them rather than washing them. For a luxurious touch, add a sprinkling of pine nuts before glazing.

Preparation time: 15 minutes
Cooking time: 10 minutes

METRIC/IMPERIAL	AMERICAN
55g/2 oz plain white flour	½ cup all-purpose flour
55g/2 oz wholemeal flour	½ cup wholewheat flour
55g/2 oz vegan margarine	¼ cup vegan margarine
30g/1 oz raw cane sugar	2 tablespoons raw cane sugar
few drops orange flower water (optional)	few drops orange flower water (optional)
4 fresh figs	4 fresh figs
4 kiwi fruit, peeled	4 kiwis, peeled
2 tablespoons apricot jam	2 tablespoons apricot jam

1 Sift the flours into a bowl, rub in the margarine to make a mixture like fine breadcrumbs, then stir in the sugar. Add the orange flower water, if using it, with enough cold water to mix to a fairly firm dough – about 2–3 tablespoons. Wrap the pastry in foil and chill for 30 minutes.

2 Roll out the pastry on a floured board and cut into 8 7.5cm (3 in) circles. Use to line lightly greased bun tins, then line with foil, fill with baking beans, and bake in the oven at 200°C/400°F (Gas Mark 6) for 10 minutes. Cool slightly, then remove the beans and foil, carefully transfer the cases to a wire rack and leave to cool.

3 Slice the figs and kiwi fruit into rings and arrange them in the pastry cases. Heat the apricot jam gently and then brush the tops of the fruit with it to glaze. Leave to cool, then eat on the same day.

TIP You can, of course, use other summer fruits, either combining different types or using just one sort. Alternatively, reduce the amount of fruit needed by putting a few spoonfuls of cream or custard in the pastry cases then arranging thin slices of fruit on top.

Wholemeal Scones

Scones with strawberry jam and clotted cream are a real summer favourite. This wholemeal version is even tastier than scones made with white flour. If you want to serve them in the traditional way, add some low-sugar jam, and a spoonful of crème fraîche.

Preparation time: 10 minutes
Cooking time: 20 minutes

METRIC/IMPERIAL	AMERICAN
225g/8 oz wholemeal flour	2 cups wholewheat flour
2 teaspoons baking powder	2 teaspoons baking powder
30g/1 oz butter or margarine	2 tablespoons butter or margarine
30g/1 oz raw cane sugar	2 tablespoons raw cane sugar
about 140ml/¼ pint milk	about ⅓ cup milk

For the topping

1 small free-range egg, beaten	1 small free-range egg, beaten
1 tablespoon raw cane sugar	1 tablespoon raw cane sugar
½ teaspoo 1 ground cinnamon	½ teaspoon ground cinnamon

1 In a bowl, sift together the flour and baking powder. Then use your fingers to rub in the butter or margarine until the mixture resembles fine breadcrumbs. Stir in the sugar.

2 Stir in just enough milk to bind the ingredients to a soft dough, then turn this out on to a floured board and kneading lightly for a few minutes. Roll out to 2cm (¾ in) and use a pastry cutter or a sharp knife to cut into circles or triangles.

3 Transfer the scones to a lightly greased baking sheet, and brush with beaten egg then sprinkle with the sugar and cinnamon. Bake in the oven at 200°C/400°F (Gas Mark 6) for 20 minutes, or until well risen and firm to touch. Leave to cool slightly. Best eaten warm.

TIP Scones don't keep well, but any that are left the following day could be toasted. A vegan version could be made by using soya instead of dairy milk and omitting the egg glaze. This basic recipe can be adapted by adding sultanas, dates, nuts and other ingredients. Try making a savoury version, too, by adding herbs and cheese.

Carrot and Banana Squares

This recipe uses banana chips for a sweet, crunchy topping that contrasts well with the moist, spicy cake itself.

Preparation time: 10 minutes
Cooking time: 45–60 minutes

METRIC/IMPERIAL	AMERICAN
115g/4 oz margarine	½ cup margarine
115g/4 oz margarine	½ cup margarine
115g/4 oz raw cane sugar	⅔ cup raw cane sugar
2 free-range eggs, beaten	2 free-range eggs, beaten
170g/6 oz carrots, grated	6 ounces carrots, grated
1 ripe banana, mashed	1 ripe banana, mashed
115g/4 oz wholemeal flour	1 cup wholewheat flour
2 level teaspoons baking powder	2 level teaspoons baking powder
½ teaspoon mixed spice	½ teaspoon mixed spice

For the topping

2 teaspoons raw cane sugar	2 teaspoons raw cane sugar
2 tablespoons banana chips	2 tablespoons banana chips

1 In a bowl, cream together the margarine and sugar. Stir in the beaten eggs, carrots and banana, mixing well.
2 Sift together the flour, baking powder and mixed spice, then combine with the other ingredients. The mixture should be fairly soft, but if it seems too moist, add another spoonful of flour.
3 Lightly grease a medium-sized square cake tin, pour in the mixture and smooth the top. Sprinkle with sugar and banana chips, breaking them into smaller pieces if necessary. Bake in the oven at 180°C/350°F (Gas Mark 4) for 45–60 minutes. To test the cake, insert a sharp knife into the centre; it will come out clean if the cake is cooked.
4 Cool briefly in the tin, then turn out on to a wire rack and leave to cool completely. Cut into squares to serve. Squares should keep for about 4 days in an airtight container.

TIP Carrot cake makes a delicious dessert when topped with cream, yogurt or, for something completely different, apple purée. Instead of grated carrot, add some puréed pumpkin to the mixture.

Nut and Honey Slices

———◆·◆———

A taste of the Middle East, these sweet, crisp slices are based on
baklava and kataifi, but are considerably lower in calories.

Preparation time: 10 minutes
Cooking time: 20–30 minutes

METRIC/IMPERIAL

115g/4 oz almonds, coarsely
chopped

4 tablespoons runny honey

140ml/¼ pint orange juice

1 teaspoon rose water (optional)

1 teaspoon mixed spice

55g/2 oz wholemeal
breadcrumbs

6 sheets filo pastry

vegetable oil

AMERICAN

1 cup coarsely chopped
almonds

4 tablespoons runny honey

⅔ cup orange juice

1 teaspoon rose-water (optional)

1 teaspoon mixed spice

1 cup wholewheat
breadcrumbs

6 sheets filo pastry

vegetable oil

1 In a bowl stir together the almonds, honey, orange juice, rose water, if using, and mixed spice. Stir in the breadcrumbs, making sure everything is well mixed.

2 Lay one sheet of filo pastry on a lightly floured board and brush with oil. Transfer to a shallow oblong cake tin and, if the pastry is too large, trim off any excess. Repeat with a second sheet of pastry, laying it over the first.

3 Spread half the nut and honey mixture evenly over the top. Cover with a further 2 sheets of filo pastry brushed with oil, then add the remaining filling and top with the final 2 sheets of pastry. Brush the top with oil.

4 Use a sharp knife to score the top into squares. Bake in the oven at 180°C/350°F (Gas Mark 4) for 20–30 minutes, or until the top begins to colour. Leave to cool briefly, then cut through the squares, and serve. preferably while still warm.

TIP Vegans can substitute syrup for the honey. Other nuts can be used instead of almonds; pistachios are particularly good. Make sure you keep the filo pastry you are not yet working with covered with a damp cloth to prevent it drying out.

Ginger Pear Bars
———◆◆———

The texture of dried pears and the taste of ginger makes a delicious combination.

Preparation time: 15 minutes
Cooking time: None

METRIC/IMPERIAL	AMERICAN
225g/8 oz dried pears	8 ounces dried pears
½ teaspoon ground cinnamon	½ teaspoon ground cinnamon
½ teaspoon ground ginger	½ teaspoon ground ginger
85g/3 oz roasted peanuts	⅔ cup roasted peanuts
1 tablespoon ginger marmalade or preserve	1 tablespoon ginger marmalade or preserve
edible rice paper	edible rice paper

1 Wash the pears and dry them thoroughly. Then mince them, or better still, purée in a food processor. Add the spices.
2 Grind the peanuts. Stir into the pears with the marmalade. The paste should be thick and fairly dry; if necessary, add more ground nuts.
3 Put a sheet of rice paper in a small, shallow cake tin, spread the pear mixture over it and press it down evenly. Top with another sheet of rice paper, pressing down again. A rolling pin ensures an even finish. Then use a sharp knife to cut into bars. If not eating them straight away, store in an airtight container in a cool place.

TIP To make these bars even more delicious, cut them into small squares, then melt a carob bar and dip the squares into it so that they are coated on one side. Allow to cool, then serve with after-dinner coffee.

Muesli Bars

V+

These tasty, crunchy bars are so quick and easy that a child could make them – and will probably be efficient at disposing of them too, just as soon as they're cool enough to handle! As it's hard to tell when they're done until they firm up, aim to undercook instead of leaving them just a minute or two longer.

Preparation time: 5 minutes
Cooking time: 15 minutes

METRIC/IMPERIAL	AMERICAN
170g/6 oz vegan margarine	¾ cup vegan margarine
4 tablespoons barley malt syrup	4 tablespoons barley malt syrup
170g/6 oz muesli	1½ cups muesli
170g/6 oz rolled oats	1½ cups rolled oats
55g/2 oz raw cane sugar	⅓ cup raw cane sugar
55g/2 oz glacé cherries, chopped	½ cup chopped candied cherries

1 Melt the margarine and syrup in a saucepan, stirring well, then set aside.
2 In a large bowl stir together the muesli, oats and sugar. Pour in the margarine and syrup and mix well, then add the cherries, making sure everything is evenly distributed.
3 Lightly grease a Swiss roll (jelly roll) tin. Spoon in the mixture, pressing it down gently and smoothing the top. Bake in the oven at 200°C/400°F (Gas Mark 6) for 15 minutes, or until golden. Mark into bars but leave to cool in the tin. Then cut along the marked lines and transfer to an airtight container.

TIP Homemade or wholefood shop-bought muesli is best as it usually contains less sugar. If using a supermarket variety, you may need to adjust the sweetening. Vegetarians could use honey instead of the syrup. Extra chopped dried fruit, nuts and seeds can also be used.

Luxury Ginger Nuts

These crisp biscuits are delicious just as they are, but you could also try serving them with ice-cream or sorbet, sandwiching them together with a lemon cream, or crumbling them over stewed fruit.

Preparation time: 10 minutes
Cooking time: 15–20 minutes

METRIC/IMPERIAL	AMERICAN
225g/8 oz wholemeal flour	2 cups wholewheat flour
2 teaspoons baking powder	2 teaspoons baking powder
1 teaspoon ground ginger	1 teaspoon ground ginger
115g/4 oz raw cane sugar	⅔ cup raw cane sugar
85g/3 oz margarine	⅓ cup margarine
4 tablespoons syrup	4 tablespoons syrup
1 small free-range egg, beaten	1 small free-range egg, beaten
2 tablespoons chopped crystallized ginger	2 tablespoons chopped crystallized ginger

1 Sift together the flour, baking powder and ground ginger. Stir in the sugar.

2 In a small saucepan, melt the margarine with the syrup. Add this to the first mixture with the egg and crystallized ginger, making sure the ginger is evenly distributed. Mix to form a dough.

3 Roll out the dough on a lightly floured board, then cut out small rounds with a pastry cutter or a cup. Place these on a greased baking tray (you may need 2), leaving space for the biscuits to spread.

4 Bake in the oven at 180°C/350°F (Gas Mark 4) for 15–20 minutes until golden but still soft. Leave to cool for a few minutes, then transfer the ginger nuts to a wire rack. They will become crisper once cold.

TIP These biscuits keep well in an airtight container, or can even be frozen, so it's worth making double the quantity. You could replace the crystallized ginger with chocolate or carob chips in half of the batch.

Apple Crumble Slices

Although rather fiddly to make, these slices are well worth the effort. The coconut makes the crumble topping especially munchy!

Preparation time: 10 minutes (plus making the apple purée)
Cooking time: 35–40 minutes

METRIC/IMPERIAL	AMERICAN
115g/4 oz wholemeal flour	1 cup wholewheat flour
2 teaspoons baking powder	2 teaspoons baking powder
55g/2 oz desiccated coconut	⅔ cup shredded coconut
85g/3 oz raw cane sugar	½ cup raw cane sugar
85g/3 oz margarine, melted	⅓ cup margarine, melted
about 285ml/½ pint apple purée (see page 40)	about 1¼ cups apple purée (see page 40)

For the topping

55g/2 oz wholemeal flour	½ cup wholewheat flour
30g/1 oz margarine	2 tablespoons margarine
55g/2 oz raw cane sugar	⅓ cup raw cane sugar
30g/1 oz desiccated coconut	⅓ cup shredded coconut

1 Sift the flour and baking powder into a bowl, stir in the coconut and sugar, then gradually add the melted margarine, mixing it in well.

2 Turn the mixture into a lightly greased Swiss roll (jelly roll) tin. Bake in the oven at 180°C/350°F (Gas Mark 4) for 10 minutes, then remove from the oven and set aside.

3 To make the crumble topping, put the flour into a bowl and rub in the margarine to make a crumb-like mixture. Stir in the sugar and coconut.

4 Make sure the apple purée is well drained, then spread it over the prepared base and top it with the crumble mixture. Bake at the same temperature for 25–30 minutes, or until the top is lightly browned. Allow to cool for a while before cutting into slices. Store in an airtight container.

TIP Though they will keep for a day or two, these slices are best eaten fresh – even warm. Top them with cream or custard for dessert. For a change, mix the apple with blackberries, or use an apricot or strawberry purée. You could also use a low-sugar jam.

Semolina Shortbread with Seeds

Make up lots of this shortbread and keep it handy for when people arrive unexpectedly, for lunch boxes and picnics, for serving with fruit salads, sorbets and ice-creams, for crumbling over purées . . .

Preparation time: 10 minutes (plus chilling)
Cooking time: 45 minutes

METRIC/IMPERIAL	AMERICAN
115g/4 oz butter or margarine	½ cup butter or margarine
55g/2 oz raw cane sugar	⅓ cup raw cane sugar
115g/4 oz wholemeal flour	1 cup wholewheat flour
55g/2 oz wholemeal semolina	½ cup wholewheat semolina
1 teaspoon poppy seeds	1 teaspoon poppy seeds
1 teaspoon sesame seeds	1 teaspoon sesame seeds
1 teaspoon sunflower seeds	1 teaspoon sunflower seeds
caster sugar (optional)	superfine sugar (optional)

1 In a bowl, cream together the butter or margarine and the sugar. Then use a knife to stir in the flour and semolina until the mixture resembles breadcrumbs. Press this together with your fingers into a firm dough.
2 Transfer to a lightly floured board and knead for a few minutes until smooth.
3 Press the mixture into a round 20cm (8 in) loose-bottomed flan tin (tart pan), or a greased and lined cake tin. Mark into 8 or 12 segments, prick the top with a fork, then sprinkle with the poppy seeds, sesame seeds and sunflower seeds, pressing them gently into the dough. Chill in the fridge for 1 hour.
4 Bake in the oven at 150°C/300°F (Gas Mark 2) for 45 minutes, or until just firm. Take care not to overcook the shortbread or it will be dry. Allow to cool in the tin, then cut or break into segments. Store in an airtight container until needed. It is traditional to sprinkle shortbread with caster sugar (superfine sugar) just before serving.

TIP Adding semolina gives shortbread a crunchier texture. If you prefer, you can make it with just wholemeal flour, or half wholemeal and half white flour. You can also use other flavourings – try adding spices, dried fruit, chopped nuts, etc.

Vitality Munch

Mixes you can pick at and munch are becoming increasingly popular. Once you could only buy them at wholefood shops – now they're available from greengrocers, supermarkets, even newsagents. They're usually prepacked and expensive, so why not make your own? The recipe below is just to give you the idea.

Preparation time: 5 minutes
Cooking time: None

METRIC/IMPERIAL	AMERICAN
115g/4 oz raisins	⅔ cup raisins
115g/4 oz dried apricots, chopped	1 cup chopped dried apricots
115g/4 oz dried figs, chopped	1 cup chopped dried figs
115g/4 oz dried apples, chopped	1 cup chopped dried apples
55g/2 oz pumpkin seeds	½ cup pumpkin seeds
225g/8 oz mixed nuts	2 cups mixed nuts
115g/4 oz flaked coconut, toasted	1⅓ cups flaked coconut, toasted
115g/4 oz banana chips	1⅓ cups banana chips
115g/4 oz carob bar, coarsely chopped	4 ounce carob bar, coarsely chopped

1   Simply mix together all the ingredients and store in a screwtop jar.

TIP This mix is full of nutrients and energy. It's best not to make up too much at one time, since cutting the fruit means not only that nutrients are soon lost but that freshness and flavour go the same way. This is why it's best to leave the nuts whole, though you could halve the larger ones, such as Brazil nuts.

Lemon Mousse

The perfect dessert – light, sharp yet sweet.

Preparation time: 10 minutes
Cooking time: 10 minutes

METRIC/IMPERIAL	AMERICAN
2 lemons	2 lemons
570ml/1 pint water	2½ cups water
2 teaspoons agar-agar	2 teaspoons agar-agar
55g/2 oz raw cane sugar	⅓ cup raw cane sugar
140ml/¼ pint crème fraîche	⅔ cup crème fraîche
55g/2 oz raw sugar chocolate, grated	2 ounces raw sugar chocolate, grated
toasted flaked almonds	toasted flaked almonds

1 Halve the lemons, then squeeze to extract the juice. Set the juice aside.
2 Bring the water to a boil in a saucepan and add the chopped peel. Lower the heat, cover the pan and simmer for 10 minutes. Strain, then dissolve the agar-agar and sugar in the hot liquid and cook for 3 minutes. Stir in the lemon juice.
3 Transfer to the fridge and leave until it begins to set. Then use a whisk to mix in the crème fraîche. Divide the mixture between 4 dishes or glasses and chill again.
4 Serve sprinkled with the grated chocolate and flaked almonds. Also good as a topping for heavier dishes such as Christmas pudding.

TIP You can use this basic recipe to make fruit jellies of all kinds. You'll find agar-agar (or gellozone, which is also made from seaweed and has similar gelling qualities) in wholefood shops.

Mixed Fruit Crumble with Cashew Cream

V+

Make this in early summer when rhubarb is at its best and needs only a little cooking. The cashew cream – smooth and not at all fatty – makes a far nicer topping than dairy cream.

Preparation time: 15 minutes
Cooking time: 35–40 minutes

METRIC/IMPERIAL	AMERICAN
225g/8 oz fresh rhubarb, cleaned and chopped	½ pound fresh rhubarb, cleaned and chopped
2 medium cooking apples, peeled, cored and chopped	2 medium cooking apples, peeled, cored and chopped
55g/2 oz raisins	⅓ cup raisins
55g/2 oz raw cane sugar, or to taste	⅓ cup raw cane sugar, or to taste
squeeze of lemon juice	squeeze of lemon juice

For the crumble

115g/4 oz wholemeal flour	1 cup wholewheat flour
½ teaspoon baking powder	½ teaspoon baking powder
½ teaspoon mixed spice	½ teaspoon mixed spice
55g/2 oz vegan margarine	¼ cup vegan margarine
55g/2 oz raw cane sugar	⅓ cup raw cane sugar

For the cashew cream

85g/3 oz cashew nuts, ground	⅔ cup cashew nuts, ground
140ml/¼ pint concentrated soya milk or soya 'cream'	⅔ cup concentrated soya milk or soya 'cream'
a little maple syrup or apple concentrate	a little maple syrup or apple concentrate

1 Put the rhubarb, apples, raisins, sugar and lemon juice into a saucepan and add a few spoonfuls of water. Cover and cook over low heat for 10 minutes, or until the fruit softens but doesn't lose its shape. Check that it doesn't dry out, adding a little more water if necessary. Transfer the mixture to an ovenproof dish.

2 To make the crumble, sift together the flour, baking powder and mixed spice, then use your fingertips to rub in the margarine. When the mixture resembles breadcrumbs, sprinkle it over the fruit. Bake in the oven at 190°C/375°F (Gas Mark 5) for 25–30 minutes, or until crisp and golden.

3 Meanwhile, make the cashew cream by combining the ground cashew nuts and soya milk – adjust the quantities if necessary to give the cream the consistency you prefer. Add just a little maple syrup or apple concentrate to sweeten it, then chill until needed. Serve the hot crumble topped with cold cream.

TIP Other fruit crumbles can be made in the same way. Try using half flour, half oats for the crumble, adding some sunflower seeds or chopped almonds if you like. You can, of course, top your crumble with dairy cream, or custard, or – for vegans – one of the many ready-made soya 'desserts' that need only to be opened and poured.

Tofu Cheesecake

V+

Cheesecakes can be almost sickeningly rich – and are certainly a dessert dieters feel they should avoid. This one is made with silken tofu, which means it is light, non-fatty, and low in calories. Enjoy!

Preparation time: 15 minutes (plus soaking overnight for the apricots and chilling time)
Cooking time: 15 minutes

METRIC/IMPERIAL	AMERICAN
For the base	**For the base**
170g/6 oz vegan digestive biscuits	6 ounces vegan digestive biscuits
55g/2 oz vegan margarine	¼ cup vegan margarine
1 teaspoon ground ginger	1 teaspoon ground ginger
30g/1 oz raw cane sugar (optional)	2 tablespoons raw cane sugar (optional)
For the filling	**For the filling**
170g/6 oz dried apricots, soaked overnight	1 cup dried apricots, soaked overnight
570ml/1 pint cold water	2½ cups cold water
1 teaspoon vanilla extract	1 teaspoon vanilla extract
6 tablespoons syrup	6 tablespoons syrup
1–2 teaspoons agar-agar	1–2 teaspoons agar-agar
455g/1 lb silken tofu, drained	2 cups silken tofu, drained
30g/1 oz flaked almonds, toasted	¼ cup flaked almonds, toasted

1 Crush the biscuits to make fine crumbs. Melt the margarine in a saucepan and stir in the biscuits, ginger and sugar, if using. Press the mixture on to the base and sides of a 17.5cm/7 in flan dish (tart pan). Set aside.

2 Drain the dried apricot pieces, place in a pan and cover with fresh water, then bring to a boil and cook for 15 minutes or until tender. Drain again.

3 In a blender combine the apricots, cold water, vanilla extract, syrup, agar-agar and tofu to make a thick cream. Pour this into the biscuit case and smooth the top.

4 Return the cheesecake to the fridge and chill until it sets firm. Decorate with flaked almonds, and serve cut into wedges.

TIP Many digestive biscuits – especially those sold in wholefood shops – are vegan, but if in doubt, check the packet. Other biscuits or breakfast cereals could be used in much the same way. Adjust the amount of agar-agar you use to make the filling soft or more firm, as preferred.

Pumpkin Puddings

V+

A lovely light alternative to the traditional heavy Christmas pudding – it's the pumpkin that makes the difference. But make a point of eating these tasty little puddings at other times of year too.

Preparation time: 20 minutes (plus standing overnight)
Cooking time: 1½–2 hours

METRIC/IMPERIAL	AMERICAN
115g/4 oz wholemeal flour	1 cup wholewheat flour
1 teaspoon baking powder	1 teaspoon baking powder
115g/4 oz dried wholemeal breadcrumbs	1 cup dried wholewheat breadcrumbs
1 teaspoon ground cinnamon	1 teaspoon ground cinnamon
½ teaspoon ground nutmeg	½ teaspoon ground nutmeg
340g/12 oz cooked pumpkin, puréed	12 ounces cooked pumpkin, puréed
55g/2 oz chopped mixed peel	⅓ cup chopped candied peel
55g/2 oz sultanas	⅓ cup sultanas
55g/2 oz dried apricots, chopped	⅓ cup chopped dried apricots
55g/2 oz dates, chopped	⅓ cup chopped dates
5 tablespoons vegetable oil	5 tablespoons vegetable oil
1 tablespoon soya flour	1 tablespoon soy flour
55g/2 oz raw cane sugar	⅓ cup raw cane sugar
55g/2 oz pecan nuts, chopped	½ cup chopped pecan nuts

1 In a bowl, sift together the flour and baking powder then add the breadcrumbs and spices. Drain the pumpkin purée well and stir it into the dry ingredients.

2 Add all the dried fruit and the vegetable oil.

3 Blend the soya flour with 2 tablespoons cold water, then add this to the other ingredients. Finally mix in the sugar and nuts. You should now have a smooth, thick paste – make sure everything is well blended.

4 Take 4 small pudding basins, ramekins or old cups, and divide the mixture between them, pressing it down well. Cover with silver foil, pleating the top to allow room for the puddings to rise. Leave overnight.

5 Stand the basins in a large ovenproof pan or dish and fill it with enough hot water to come halfway up the sides. Bake in the oven at 170°C/325°F (Gas Mark 3) for about 2 hours – watch that the pan doesn't boil dry. You can serve the puddings at once, keep them in the fridge for a day or two, or freeze them.

TIP You can buy pumpkin purée in tins, but if you have a freezer, you could prepare your own in late autumn then freeze it until needed.

Danish Apple Pudding

Here's a simple but unusual way to turn apple purée into the kind of dessert that will have everyone scraping their bowls clean.

Preparation time: 15 minutes
Cooking time: 15 minutes

METRIC/IMPERIAL	AMERICAN
455g/1 lb cooking apples, peeled, cored and sliced	1 pound cooking apples, peeled, cored and sliced
1 tablespoon chopped lemon rind	1 tablespoon chopped lemon rind
½ teaspoon ground cinnamon	½ teaspoon ground cinnamon
¼ teaspoon ground cloves	¼ teaspoon ground cloves
115g/4 oz raw cane sugar	⅔ cup raw cane sugar
55g/2 oz sultanas (optional)	⅓ cup sultanas (optional)
30g/1 oz almonds, chopped (optional)	¼ cup chopped almonds (optional)
55g/2 oz butter or margarine	¼ cup butter or margarine
170g/6 oz wholemeal breadcrumbs	3 cups wholewheat breadcrumbs

For the topping	**For the topping**
140ml/¼ pint whipping cream	⅔ cup whipping cream
3 tablespoons soured cream	3 tablespoons soured cream
1 teaspoon vanilla extract	1 teaspoon vanilla extract
2 tablespoons icing sugar	2 tablespoons confectioner's sugar

1 Put the apples into a pan with the lemon rind, spices and half the sugar. Cover and cook gently until the apples collapse, adding a drop of water if necessary (though the purée should be as dry as possible to retain flavour). Sieve or mash to make a smooth purée. Stir in the sultanas and almonds, if using.

2 Melt the butter or margarine in a saucepan and stir in the breadcrumbs, frying them until they begin to crisp up. Stir in the remaining sugar.

3 In a glass serving bowl alternate layers of apple purée and breadcrumbs, finishing with apple purée.

4 Whip the cream until thick then stir in the soured cream, vanilla extract and sugar. Spread or pipe this over the apple mixture and serve.

TIP *Make up extra apple purée and keep for use in other recipes. Packed in individual containers, it freezes well.*

Frozen Peach Yogurt

Lower in calories than ice-cream, with a creamy texture and unusually tangy flavour, frozen yogurt is a taste well worth acquiring. Try it flavoured with peaches, then experiment with other fruit such as blackberry and apple, banana or pineapple. It can also be flavoured with coffee, chocolate or natural essences.

Preparation time: 10 minutes
Cooking time: None

METRIC/IMPERIAL	AMERICAN
425ml/¾ pint plain yogurt	2 cups plain yogurt
2 large ripe peaches	2 large ripe peaches
115g/4 oz raw cane sugar	⅔ cup raw cane sugar

1 Pour the yogurt into a shallow freezing tray, cover, and freeze until just becoming mushy.
2 Peel the peaches, remove the stones and chop the flesh. Then put into a blender with the sugar and blend to a smooth purée. Mix with the semi-frozen yogurt, stirring well.
3 Return the mixture to the fridge for a short time before serving.

TIP Like ice-cream, frozen yogurt can be used as the base for a wide range of sundaes. Use tall glasses and add fresh fruit, nuts, maple syrup or honey, fruit purées – and a topping of whipped cream if you're feeling indulgent.

Pineapple Ice-Cream

V+

An ice-cream that doesn't contain any cream? True. Made with one of the new soya creams, it could almost be the real thing, except that it's so much better for you.

Preparation time: 10 minutes (plus chilling time)
Cooking time: None

METRIC/IMPERIAL	AMERICAN
395g/14 oz can pineapple pieces in natural juice	medium can pineapple pieces in natural juice
200ml/⅓ pint soya 'cream' or concentrated soya milk	¾ cup soya 'cream' or concentrated soya milk
2 tablespoons orange juice	2 tablespoons orange juice
55g/2 oz raw cane sugar	⅓ cup raw cane sugar
extra pineapple pieces or crushed pineapple to serve	extra pineapple pieces or crushed pineapple to serve

1 Drain the pineapple pieces. Put all the ingredients (except the extra pineapple) into a blender and blend until smooth.
2 Pour the mixture into a freezing tray and freeze until just firm. Beat well, then freeze until set. Serve topped with pineapple pieces or a little crushed pineapple.

TIP You can now buy an excellent soya 'cream' that works well in this recipe, though concentrated soya milk makes a good substitute. Both versions make a fairly rich tasting ice-cream. Substitute other fruits – mangoes are wonderful. Or, of course, you could use flavourings such as vanilla or almond essence with some chopped nuts. For a more exotic version, add desiccated (shredded) coconut.

Truffles

V+

Serve these truffles with after-dinner coffee, at parties or as a nibble. Or pack them into a pretty box, and give them as a gift.

Preparation time: 10 minutes
Cooking time: None

METRIC/IMPERIAL	AMERICAN
55g/2 oz dates, finely chopped	½ cup finely chopped dates
55g/2 oz raisins, finely chopped	⅓ cup finely chopped raisins
115g/4 oz nuts, finely chopped	¾ cup finely chopped nuts
55g/2 oz vegan wholemeal cake crumbs	1 cup vegan wholewheat cake crumbs
4 tablespoons peanut butter	4 tablespoons peanut butter
icing sugar	confectioners' sugar

For coating

cocoa powder	cocoa powder
desiccated coconut	desiccated coconut
marzipan	marzipan

1 Make sure the dried fruit and nuts are finely chopped or mashed, then stir them together with the cake crumbs. Mix in the peanut butter. If the mixture seems too dry to hold together, either use more peanut butter or add a little fruit juice.

2 Dust your hands with a little sugar to prevent sticking and divide the mixture into about 12 balls, then put them in the fridge for about 1 hour.

3 You can cover them all in just one kind of coating, but using a variety makes the truffles both look and taste more interesting. Roll 4 of them gently in the cocoa powder and another 4 in coconut. Roll out some marzipan and shape this around the remaining 4. Put each into a paper sweet case when prepared, cover them and leave in the fridge until needed.

TIP These will keep for a few days if stored in a cool place. They're also a fun thing for children to try their hands at – if you can keep them from eating the ingredients as they work!

PLANNING YOUR MENU

Spontaneous meals can be fun occasionally, but it's generally advisable to have some idea of what you intend to serve. Spending ten minutes deciding what might go with what, then checking that you have the right ingredients and equipment, can save you time and money, and reduce the possibility of last-minute panics in the kitchen. This is especially true if it's to be a meal at which vegetarians and non-vegetarians will sit down together. And though the prospect might sound daunting, once you get into the habit of matching vegetarian and meat or fish dishes, you'll find it comes automatically.

Below are two lists. The first is of more conventional dishes in which a key ingredient is either meat or fish, and alongside each one is a suggested dish for vegetarians. They have been carefully chosen to match the main dish as closely as possible, though not always to imitate its flavour. More important are such aspects as cooking time and method, possible accompaniments (which should ideally be suitable for serving with both versions of the main course), and so on.

Just a few of the alternatives have been suggested in order to show how junk foods can be replaced with wholefoods. Not strictly necessary for vegetarians, of course, but not a bad idea either.

Feel free to adapt the recipes to suit what you have in stock and your family's tastes. And above all, remember that the aim is to enjoy your meals and time together!

Matchmaker Meals

Breakfast

When everyone else has:	Vegetarian wholefood alternative:
Supermarket cereals	Banana Wheatgerm Muesli (page 38)
	Barley Malt Granola (page 32)
Bacon sandwich	Tempeh Sandwich (page 39)
Waffles with fried bacon	Sunflower Waffles with Apple Purée (page 40)
Kippers	Scrambled Tofu on Toast (page 34)
Traditional fried breakfast	Vegetarian Fried Breakfast (page 46)
Stewed prunes	Dried Fruit Compote with Tahini Cream (page 44)

Snacks, Starters

When everyone else has:	Vegetarian wholefood alternative:
Pâté (liver, fish etc)	Aubergine Hazelnut Pâté (page 50)
	Blue Cheese Pâté Roll (page 53)
	Hummus with Avocado (page 166)
Fish fingers	Tofu Fingers (page 56)
Corned beef or ham and coleslaw	Nutmeat with Pineapple Coleslaw (page 64)
Avocado with prawns	Avocado with Pink Grapefruit (page 52)
Curried chicken salad	Curried Egg and Celery Salad (page 57)
Spinach and tuna salad	Spinach, Potato and Tofu Salad (page 62)
Fish chowder	Sweetcorn Chowder (page 66)
Chinese cabbage and pork soup	Chinese Cabbage Egg-Drop Soup (page 70)
Beef burgers	Aduki Bean Burgers (page 74)
Ham, chicken or tuna omelette	Spanish Omelette (page 92)
Chicken nuggets	Seitan Nuggets (page 93)
Scampi in batter	Pakora Vegetables (page 178)

Everyday Meals

When everyone else has:	Vegetarian wholefood alternative:
Meat or fish risotto	Lentil and Walnut Risotto (page 88)
	Millet Pilaff (page 176)
Sausage toad in the hole	Toad in the Hole (page 90)
Shepherd's pie	Beany Shepherd's Pie (page 82)
Quiche Lorraine	Smoked Cheddar and Broccoli Quiche (page 94)
Fried chops/escalopes etc.	Fried Goat's Cheese (page 180)
Meat loaf	Rice and Cheese Loaf (page 115)
Tuna Florentine	Eggs Florentine (page 96)
Chili con carne	Chili Non Carne (page 86)
Beef cobbler	Marrow Cobbler (page 124)
Stew and dumplings	'Beef' Hotpot (page 102)
Macaroni with ham	Mediterranean Pasta Bake with Tofu (page 100)
Meat suet pudding	Savoury Suet Pudding (page 84)
Corned Beef Hash	Pan Haggarty (page 158)
Ham pancakes	Hazelnut Pancakes Peperonata (page 162)
Vegetables stuffed with meat	Mixed Stuffed Vegetables (page 174)

Dinner Party Specials

When everyone else has:	*Vegetarian wholefood alternative:*
Lamb moussaka	Tofu Moussaka (page 106)
Meat dolmas	Lettuce Parcels with Creamy Carrot Sauce (page 110)
Meat lasagne	Courgette (Zucchini) Lasagne (page 118)
Couscous with meat	Vegetable Couscous (page 134)
Ham or chicken roulade	Cauliflower Cheese Roulade (page 104)
Noodles with tomatoes and tuna	Pasta with Pesto and Sun-Dried Tomatoes (page 138)
Ham, chicken or tuna pancakes	Hazelnut Pancakes Peperonata (page 162)
Beef curry	Mixed Vegetable Curry with Coconut Sauce (page 144)
Tagliatelle with meat balls	Tagliatelle with Spinach and Ricotta Balls (page 122)
Stroganoff with meat	Mixed Mushroom Stroganoff (page 108)
Sunday roast	Wheat Berry and Lentil Bake (page 136)
Venison Pie	Bean and Aubergine Pies (page 98)
Stir-Fry with chicken or prawn	Vegetable and Cashew Stir-Fry (page 152)

For Picnics or Patio Eating

When everyone else has:	Vegetarian wholefood alternative:
Meat kebabs	Vegetarian Kebabs (page 126)
Meat-filled tacos	Mushroom Tacos (page 130)
Scotch eggs	Potato Scotch Eggs (page 54)
Ham or tuna pizza	Fennel and Mozzarella Pizza (page 168)
Cornish pasties	Vegetarian Cornish Pasties (page 76)
Veal and ham pies	Bean and Aubergine (Eggplant) Pies (page 150)
Jacket Potatoes with meat topping	Jacket Potatoes with vegetarian fillings (pages 148–151)

For Christmas

When everyone else has:	*Vegetarian wholefood alternative:*
Roast turkey	Three-Nut Loaf En Croûte with Cranberry Sauce (page 120)
	Aubergine and Feta Filo Pie (page 146)
Baked ham	Savoury Cheesecake (page)
	Layered Pancake Pie (page 112)
Christmas pudding	Christmas Pumpkin Puddings (page 000)
Brandy butter	Lemon Mousse (page 199)

INDEX